SAVVY
LEADERSHIP

Ariel,

Wishing you great
success in 2017
& beyond!

Cam Tripp

Ariel,

Wishing you great
Success in 2017
& beyond!

Dan Trigg

SAVVY LEADERSHIP

HOW TO INSPIRE ENGAGEMENT AND IGNITE HIGH PERFORMANCE

CAM TRIPP

Dedication

To my wife, Jennifer, and children, Gabriel and Fiona, because they inspire me to make the world a more engaging place.

Acknowledgements

When I first started this project, I remember thinking, "Writing a book is just like writing a really long paper." Then, as I got into it, I realized that it truly takes a team of people to pull it off.

There are countless people who have influenced my thinking about people and leadership over the years and to that team of people, thank you. I'd like to especially thank the following people:

- My wife, Jennifer, for not only being an amazing friend and wife, but also for being my proofreader, blindspotter, challenger, and encourager.

- My kids, Gabriel and Fiona, who bring so much joy and energy to my life. They are a constant reminder of the importance of investing in people who are learning to be the next generation of leaders.

- My mom, dad, and brother. I am so fortunate to come from a family of hardworking writers, educators and leadership developers. Thank you for the real world education growing up.

- My in-laws for their generosity to pitch in to make our family life work while I had to go offline to research and write.

- My informal think tank of peers whose feedback along the way has helped me to steer this project in the right direction.

- Developmental editors Floyd Largent and Jeff Hayden. Thank you for your investment, feedback and guidance on the content flow.

- Copy editor Robin Lemke. Thank you for lending your attention to detail and love for writing to this book.

- Permissions editor Adele Hutchinson. Thank you for guiding me through the process that was so overwhelming at the start.

- Interior layout designer Lorie DeWorken. Thank you for transforming my manuscript into a thoughtfully crafted book.

- Cover design team Alan Dino Hebel and Ian Koviak. People do judge a book by its cover, so thank you for making this book come alive on the outside and for humoring me with my creative ideas.

- My friends who have encouraged me with great interest all along the way – thank you for believing.

- The baristas at the coffee shop at Fifth and Main Street in Downtown Edmonds. Thank you for my daily (frequently more) dose of encouragement and the coffee to keep me going.

- Thanks to God for guiding me through this project and through life.

I…am…grateful.

TABLE OF CONTENTS

CHAPTER 1
Introduction

"If your actions inspire others to dream more, learn more,
do more and become more, you are a leader."

—JOHN QUINCY ADAMS,
THE SIXTH PRESIDENT OF THE UNITED STATES

Savvy Leadership is the fast-track playbook for extraordinary leadership in the modern world, where some things just don't work the same way they used to before the economic crises and rapid rate of change in the early 21st century.

This book is based on the fundamental notion that **how you lead matters**. It matters in terms of results; it matters to your clients and vendors, and it matters far more than you may realize to the people you're working with. And by the way—it matters to your friends and families, too, since they're the ones who experience the aftereffects of your work day, whether positive or negative. I'm sure each of us could testify to having friends who complain about their jobs because they have a leader who creates a dynamic that squelches any opportunity for them to enjoy their work. On the other hand, we all know people who really enjoy their jobs; and when you get curious enough to ask why, you often discover it's because they appreciate the way their leader does *their* job.

At its core, leadership is about guiding people across a gap to a new result. This can happen formally or informally. It can happen with a title, or without one. It can be tangible (e.g., increased efficiency or production) or intangible (commitment and morale). It takes courage and skill to do this well. While courage is a prerequisite for effective leadership, savvy leaders don't have to rely on it as much because they already know how to lead through challenges. They have confidence because of their leadership competence.

Think about doing something challenging for which you had little competence. When I was a kid, I learned how to ski. My friend was a much more advanced skier than I was and he took me to the top of a black diamond run at Squaw Valley, CA called *Headwall*. As we rode up the chairlift, my friend kept saying "yard sale" referring to people who were wiping out and leaving their goggles, skis, and poles, scattered on the steep slope. I laughed along with him, but when we got to the top of the run and I looked over the rim—panic set in. It took all of the courage I could muster to go down that run because I had very little confidence in my skiing competence. Once my competence improved, going down that run became both a challenge and fun. A similar thing happens with leadership. Once people know the "how" part of effective leadership, they can rely more on their competence than their courage.

Anyone can supervise—all you need is a set of rules and a clipboard. Anyone can manage—all you need is a title and a willingness to exercise authority. To be a Savvy Leader—to motivate, to inspire, to create a sense of purpose and mission, to not only communicate but to engage and build meaningful professional relationships—takes a lot more.

But the results for you, for your company, and most importantly for your employees, are definitely worth it.

Want to become a new kind of leader? Want to become the type of leader your employees not only want but deserve?

I'll show you how.

CHAPTER 2

The Savvy Leader

"Your problem is to bridge the gap which exists between where you are now and the goal you intend to reach."

—EARL NIGHTINGALE,
AMERICAN AUTHOR, SPEAKER, AND RADIO PERSONALITY

To understand the importance of Savvy Leadership, let's look at how leadership plays out in the real world.

In the UK "Mind the Gap" is posted at all of the subway stations, referring to the gap between the platform and the train.

A similar reminder should be posted at the desk of every leader and in every conference room, because leaders are constantly crossing gaps. The Savvy Leadership J-Curve shown below provides a simple way to visualize the impact on dynamics, and subsequent results that a leader creates by the way they lead across the gap.

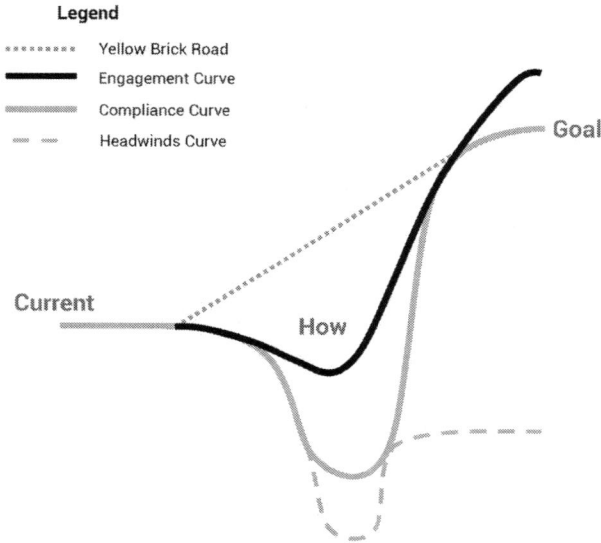

Legend

········· Yellow Brick Road

▬▬▬ Engagement Curve

▬▬▬ Compliance Curve

▭ ▭ Headwinds Curve

Goal

Current

How

On the left side of the gap is the current state of your team or business. The right side represents your goal. In-between is the journey you take to reach your goal. How you lead from the current state to your goal will determine the dynamic of the journey, and your team's collective ability to accomplish the goal.

There are three main leadership paths across the gap.

First, let's acknowledge the dotted diagonal line. That's the yellow brick road of leadership: the assumption that when we're given a goal, the pathway to results is simple with no downside. But it's unrealistic in 99 percent of leadership situations—because, well, stuff happens. There's a natural downside here, and how we lead through the dip sets the dynamic with the team.

A more realistic scenario is the solid light gray curve, we'll call the **"compliance curve."** It's the dynamic most often created by leaders who lack the leadership savvy to do otherwise. People will do their jobs, but not much else. The dip represents issues we encounter while leading our team across the gap. Unfortunately, what happens far too often is that when leaders see the downside of the dip, they imagine the trouble they may get into with *their* leader. Instead of leading for engagement in the midst of challenge, they revert to what feels safe, powerful, and productive: that is, driving harder from a base of fear and positional authority, which leads to the dashed gray path with a deeper dip I call the "**headwinds curve**."

This approach makes team members feel disempowered and disrespected, which feeds disengagement and resistance. When a leader sees the disengagement, they often do the exact wrong thing: they come down harder on their team members, almost as if they've adopted the pirate's motivational motto that "The beatings will continue until morale improves." It easily becomes a downward spiral. The outcome is then in jeopardy, and may even end in a worse place than where the project started from—leading to a reorganization, good people quitting, or the leader responsible being "given the opportunity to pursue other passions."

The dynamic that Savvy Leaders seek to create is the black **engagement curve**, which is focused on leading for continual engagement and motivation, even in the midst of challenges. It doesn't eliminate the downside of the J-Curve, but it has the effect of minimizing it, while also increasing the odds of meeting or even exceeding the goal and ending with a higher upside.

As a leader, you get to choose which curve you create by how you lead your team. If you chose the engagement curve, then you need to commit to it and be intentional about it every single day. It can't be a hit-or-miss, occasional thing; it's all or nothing.

As we look at the core concepts of Savvy Leadership in this book, a central question we'll examine is: "If I use this leadership concept, which J-Curve will I end up with?" The analysis of this question is critical to building a leadership approach that enhances engagement and ignites high-performance results.

Now, let's define what Savvy Leadership really is. I chose the word "Savvy" very purposefully. When you look up the word in the dictionary, you see associated words like "street-smart," "shrewd," "perceptive," "practical wisdom," and "experienced." It's often used in contexts such as, "The new guy is very tech-savvy," or "That person doesn't have very good business savvy." Being savvy is a compliment because it means that you understand something from a very pragmatic perspective. You know how things work, and you know how to adjust to be effective.

The working definition of Savvy Leadership that we'll use in this book is:

Savvy Leadership: an approach to leadership that increases awareness, enhances engagement, reduces headwinds, and optimizes for results.

Have you ever seen a leader who works like that? When you do, isn't it like an extra dose of oxygen in the room? Everyone breathes easier, because such leaders not only impact the people on their team, they're also able to influence others without authority—a critical competency in the modern work world of flatter, more geographically diverse organizations.

Let's drill down on the Savvy Leadership definition. Savvy Leaders aren't just aware; they are *keenly* aware. That level of awareness enables them to monitor and adjust for engagement and effectiveness, instead of being locked into one understanding and one work mode. If you've ever been a coach, teacher, or parent, then you know that there's no one-size-fits-all approach to effective leadership. Different approaches are required in different circumstances and with different people. Those who think otherwise are condemning themselves to ineffectual careers. Because of their keen awareness, Savvy Leaders know how and when to adjust, and even re-adjust.

It's not unlike fishing. If you just go to a river and cast your line, good luck with that. You might catch some fish, but you need to know the behavior of fish, the currents, and different depths of the river in order to maximize success—catch more fish and the kinds you want by arming yourself with the right kind of information. Savvy Leaders aren't just focused on results, but also on the pathway required to get there. Their default leadership mode is to enhance engagement. The concept of engagement is key. While there are various definitions of engagement, we define employee engagement as follows—

Employee Engagement: the level of commitment and motivation to work hard and give discretionary effort.

Leaders who enhance engagement reap the rewards of employees who, by their own choice, want to give extra effort to drive results. The good news and the bad news are one and the same: according to Gallup, approximately 70 percent of the employee engagement factor is due to the leader's management style.[1]

In other words, **how you lead matters.** You'll see this point repeated again and again throughout this book because truly Savvy Leadership always circles back around to it. The more your leadership fosters dynamics where engagement can thrive, the more of a positive impact it will have on performance because people are deliberately choosing to volunteer more effort. Why? *Because the Savvy Leader creates a dynamic where they want to.*

In addition to engagement, Savvy Leaders are also proactive about reducing headwinds, that is, things that create additional hassles or friction in the pursuit of a goal. Over a career spent working with hundreds of organizations, a common theme I've heard from people is that they would love their job a whole lot more if their leader wasn't making it so difficult. Leaders have the ability to enhance engagement, but they also have the power to create unnecessary toil and difficulty, which are perceived as headwinds to results. Many unaware leaders mistakenly believe that any positive results they achieve are because of their command-and-control leadership approach, not in spite of it. The truth is, they just happen to be fortunate enough to have some people who will work hard despite poor leadership, but that's not a reliable or sustainable plan in the modern world.

In doing the things that are necessary to develop awareness, enhance engagement, and reduce headwinds, Savvy Leaders are also doing small things to optimize their results. These are the tipping-point items that provide the extra impetus and energy needed to accomplish results. We'll explore them later in the book.

So, how do Savvy Leaders develop the dynamics of the engagement J-Curve?

This was dramatically illustrated to me recently when I took my family to a Seattle Mariners baseball game at Safeco Field. It was a typical overcast spring day. The massive retractable roof was open, but sure enough, by the third inning, it began to rain, so they closed the roof.

Watching the roof close is impressive. It covers over nine acres and weighs in at 22 million pounds—and it's right over your head. I imagined that there must be some gigantic diesel generator in the basement of the outfield powering the movement of the roof. But later, I came to find out that instead of *one* engine powering it, there are 96 little ten horsepower electric motors, all working together to move the massive structure so quietly that unless you look up, you might not even realize it's closing.[2]

In a very similar sense, this is what Savvy Leaders do. They realize that there are many, sometimes seemingly little things, that they do or don't do every day that has a cumulative effect on the engagement levels of their teams. Savvy Leaders understand the multi-dimensional leadership aspect required to drive engagement and high-performance; but beyond that insight, they also know how to do it, and they do so with consistency. For some it comes naturally; the rest of us could use some guidance.

The best leaders have a philosophy or "playbook" of leadership that guides their interactions, creating a repeatable pathway for high performance—just as many noteworthy sports coaches have a leadership philosophy that guides how they work with their players to drive results. Two modern examples are Phil Jackson, who coached the Chicago Bulls to multiple championships, and Pete Carroll, who coached teams to national championships in both college and pro football. Both are very Savvy Leaders.

Throughout this book, you'll no doubt experience many new insights, while having at least some of your previous knowledge validated and refreshed. The real value, however, is realized when you bring it all together to lead in a way that increases awareness, enhances engagement, reduces headwinds, and optimizes for results, just as Jackson and Carroll learned to do.

Which raises the question, what does Savvy Leadership look like in the workplace?

In my work as a consultant, I've had the opportunity to see many different types of leaders in action. While many were great (and some were not), there's one who always comes to mind as the exemplar of Savvy Leadership in action. When I first met him, he was a district manager of a national retail company. It was evident that he wholeheartedly believed in the notion that leading for engagement would pay off in developing a high-performance team. He constantly did the little things to engage and motivate his team. It worked, and he got promoted to regional VP. He led his new team the same way—only this time the economy hit the wall and went into recession. He could have easily have slipped into a command-and-control mode, as many of his colleagues did during that crisis time; but instead, he kept doing the things he needed to do to keep the engagement levels on his team high. They worked hard to hit their goals. They didn't hit all of them, but in comparison to his colleagues, his team's performance was a positive anomaly. When the carnage of the recession was over, the company reorganized and he was promoted to Chief Operating Officer. Everyone cheered his success!

This book is structured to follow the definition I outlined earlier for Savvy Leadership. There are four sections, just as there are four components to the definition. I encourage you to keep a notepad next to you as you read. Think about a situation that you need to lead in, and create your plan for using what you've learned. (You can use the Leadership Planner in the Resources section at the back of the book to create your plan.) Take the time to work through the Action Steps I've included at the end of each chapter. Some you can put into action immediately—and doing so will instantly make you a better, more engaged, and more effective leader.

By the end of the book, you'll have a new playbook, and a plan to put what you learned into action. And with time and effort, you will become a new kind of leader: A Savvy Leader.

SECTION
ONE

INCREASING AWARENESS

- Situational Awareness
- Cultural Awareness
- People Awareness

CHAPTER 3
Situational and Cultural Awareness

"Let us not look back in anger, nor forward in fear,
but around in awareness."

—JAMES THURBER,
AMERICAN AUTHOR

When my daughter was in preschool, she and her classmates had a graduation ceremony at the end of the year. Not only was it the kids' last day in preschool, but it happened to be the last day of this particular teacher's 34-year teaching career. We felt privileged to witness her final hour of dedication to her students. As the parents and grandparents lined the back of the classroom, we watched in amazement as she kept all twenty kids in learning mode the entire time. This teacher wasn't going to slack off in the last hour of her career; she was going to finish strong.

Later, one of the parents asked her, "How do you do that? We only have two kids at home, and we can't even do what you just did with twenty."

She smiled a knowing smile and asked, "Do you want to know the key to effective teaching?" We all nodded (somewhat desperately), and she said simply, "Monitor and adjust." It's the key to effectiveness in the classroom, the key to effectiveness as a leader—and the key to effectiveness in life.

Awareness is the foundation of effective leadership. Just as knowing the weather forecast provides you with information about what to wear for the day, awareness as a leader provides you with the information you need to make savvy adjustments to be more effective and to drive engagement.

The starting place of awareness is knowing how to develop it. The field of epistemology looks at the question, "How do you know what you know?" A key finding is that you see what you know. For example, if you're thinking about buying a new car, you'll probably start to notice that make and model of car more often when you're driving around. It's not because there are magically more of that kind of car on the road, it's because it's on your radar. If you're buying a Honda, you'll soon learn the differences between the EX, LX, and Touring models. If you've never owned a Honda and aren't thinking about buying one, those probably wouldn't register for you as significant—because again, you see what you know.

This is why successful salespeople educate their customers—so they know the value of an option beyond the base model/price.

Another example is right down the road from you. Have you ever noticed those seemingly random blue reflectors in the middle of the road? Do you know why they're there?

They mark the location of fire hydrants on the side of the road so firefighters can find them quickly in an emergency. Now you'll see those blue reflectors everywhere, because you see what you know!

There are so many things you can focus your awareness on in business, but in addition to the actual business, Savvy Leaders focus on developing awareness based on three types of variables: Situational, Cultural, and People. Each is like a key puzzle piece that provides you with a better picture of the dynamics that you encounter and create as you lead. Awareness is a force multiplier, like having the right equipment and intel in a military encounter. When properly focused, it can make you much more powerful and effective.

Situational Awareness

The game of football is a prime example of the awareness-effective action connection. Long before the teams step onto the field to play each other, effective teams have been in the film room, studying game films of their opponents to improve their awareness. Among other things, they study the defense schemes and offensive strategies of their opponent. Then, during the game, the quarterback walks up to the line, looks at the defensive configuration, and, if the play he's planning to run doesn't have a good chance of success, he'll call an "audible" to change the play to one that might be more effective. Some of the best quarterbacks in history weren't the most physically gifted athletes, but were incredibly effective, nonetheless, because their awareness was a force multiplier that enabled them to be more effective than their more physically gifted peers.

Peyton Manning is a good example of this. Even when he was far beyond his physical prime, he was still highly recruited and effective when his contract expired with the Colts in his mid-30s, which is elderly in football years. He landed at the Broncos and used his football savvy to take them all the way to a victory in Super Bowl 50.

In the field of education, a meta-study was done to determine what made school principals most effective. The researchers looked at a whole host of factors, including where the principals received their educations, the length of their careers, and their personalities. The number one factor of effective principals was *situational awareness*. They had a keen sense of what was going on in their school. They knew what was happening between administrators, teachers, staff, students, and parents. This situational awareness fed right into the second most important factor, *flexibility*. Their awareness provided them with a fuller picture of what was going on, and they then adjusted for the situation in order to be more effective. They moved away from a one-size-fits-all approach (which never really fits anyone) to a savvier and more nuanced approach that adapts to situations, and it paid off in fostering a high-engagement/high-performance atmosphere.[3]

This wisdom can be applied to business situations as well.

Meiying is a consultant at a large consulting company. Typically, she's brought in to provide leadership for client projects. In working with the client, she has to be able to influence both up and down, and to learn to navigate the sometimes murky waters of stated and implied responsibility, as well as competing and often conflicting agendas. Though she knows what to look for to build her awareness, she has to do it quickly. In addition to doing all the normal discovery a consultant would do to learn about a client, she works hard to find someone in the client's organization who can provide her with more internal, behind-the-scenes awareness of issues so she can be proactive and work with the true reality. She also partners with this person to run things by her to get a sense for how they would be received, and to get recommendations for adjustments. The relationship with this person is key to her ability to lead effectively, saving time, money, and frustration while doing the things necessary to enhance engagement and deliver results.

Cultural Awareness

Just as you find different cultures in different parts of the world, you also find different work cultures, depending on what organization, division, or even team you're working with. Understanding their unique culture enables you to proactively make adjustments to be more effective.

Max is a trainer for a large consulting company. Early in his career, he was facilitating a workshop at a large high-tech company. He knew what the ideal outcomes were for the client, but neglected to consider how he should adjust the workshop to better match their organizational culture. He started by diligently following the facilitator manual, to ensure he was covering all the content. He mistakenly assumed that because they were so engineering-minded, they might need some extra time to deconstruct and process the content.

Quite the opposite. This was a high-performance group full of very bright people who didn't want to go slow. During the first break, the team leader pulled him aside and anxiously requested that he quicken the pace, explaining that the audience was used to rapidly processing information. Max floored the accelerator pedal on the workshop's pace, but it was too little too late. Ultimately, the feedback wasn't good. He would have been much more effective from the start had he spent more time beforehand doing due diligence regarding the reality of the culture that he was going to be working with, and having already made adjustments from the start.

A helpful way of understanding organizational culture is by using the iceberg analogy.

The "**surface culture**" is the part of the iceberg above the water—how we *say* we things get done. This includes mission statements, policies, structure and hierarchy, annual reports, stated values, official memos, and even official job interview responses. Then there's the "**deep culture**"—the bulk of the iceberg that lies underneath the water which is how things *actually* get done. This includes shortcuts, politics, loyalties, pace, degree of engagement and effort, attitudes, beliefs, perceptions, unwritten rules, assumptions, feelings, group norms, informal networks, etc. Deep culture is a much more powerful driver of behavior and performance than surface culture.

Jeff was a relatively new supervisor when he came up with what he thought was a great plan to improve overall productivity by moving a crew to a different shift on an open production line. The inconvenience to the crew was considerable, but the payoff seemed worth it to him.

The crew disagreed. They didn't want to change shifts. They didn't want to be forced to rework family schedules and family responsibilities... and they told him so.

He heard them, but he didn't *listen*. Instead, he held firm. Great leaders make tough decisions, he thought, and do whatever it takes to get results. Plus, he was afraid he would look weak if he backed down.

It turns out Jeff had that backward.

Sure, his new shift rotation worked on paper. It even worked, to a degree, in practice. But it wreaked havoc on the family lives of a number of great employees. So he met with the crew and said, "I know you didn't think this would work, and you were right. I was wrong. Let's move you back to your original shift."

He felt terrible. He felt stupid. He was sure he'd lost any respect his employees had for him.

It turns out he was wrong about that, too. Later one employee said, "I didn't really know you, but the fact that you were willing to admit you were wrong told me everything I needed to know."

When you're wrong, say you're wrong. You won't lose respect. You'll gain it (unless you're wrong too frequently). Sometimes a decision should be based on more than analysis, logic, and reasoning, because every decision must eventually be carried out not by spreadsheets or databases or applications, but by people. In this company's case, maintaining a positive work-life balance was just as—if not more—important than making hard-nosed business decisions.

And that's why culture can sometimes matter more than analysis. Understanding the current culture—and learning to work within it before you try to dramatically change it—is what Savvy Leaders do. Leadership should be data driven, but great leadership is often subjective and intangible. If your employees don't agree with you, ask why, but don't ask just so you can defend your position. Ask in order to learn. You know things your employees don't know, and they know things you don't know—until you truly listen to what they say.

Although Jeff had learned a painful lesson, he had his eyes wide open as he moved forward.

One of the philosophical questions many people wrestle with at this point is, "Should I work with the culture, or work to *change* the culture?" The answer is "Yes!" Savvy Leaders are aware of the deep organizational culture that they're operating in, and they use their savviness to make culturally relevant adjustments. Without those adjustments, it's easy to trigger unnecessary headwinds. With those adjustments, you increase your odds of securing the commitment and engagement necessary to make great things happen. It's important to keep in mind that understanding and working with the current culture doesn't mean you've fully adopted the culture, or "gone native," but you do understand it and make adjustments in how you work with it, just as you would on an overseas/cross-cultural assignment.

Each person is also a steward of the culture, some to greater degrees than others. The motto of Seattle Pacific University is, "Engage the Culture, Change the World." The order of that motto is purposeful. It's very difficult to change anything unless you've first understood and engaged the culture as it is. That provides you with the platform of understanding to make changes. The higher you are in the organization, the more influence you have in shaping the culture that cascades from leadership. Even if you're not at the top of the hierarchy or are an individual contributor, you still have the stewardship to shape the culture in your sphere of influence. It begins with the force multiplier of understanding what the deep culture really is, then adapting your influence and leadership approach based on that reality before pushing the envelope to create a healthier culture.

Sophie is a junior consultant at a large consulting company. It's a male-dominated culture, and at the beginning, she felt out of place and certainly out of the inner circle. Instead of getting frustrated by this, she became curious and adopted the mindset of a sociologist to study the culture there. She listened to the things her colleagues talked about, especially their banter, and came to realize that much of it revolved around sports and player stats. Though she grew up playing sports, the whole world of player stats was like a foreign language to her. But she was determined to learn the language, and even downloaded an app on her smartphone so that every morning on her way to work on the train, she could see the updated stats for the local teams.

Pretty soon she became familiar with it all and one day, as the informal sports banter was taking place at the beginning of the meeting, she chimed in. At first, there was a stunned reaction; they paused, then kept going. She did it again the next day, and they realized she was actually into it. She then took it to the next level, and with the help of a friend, created her own fantasy team. At the next meeting, she chimed in again. The men she worked with asked her how she knew all this, and she said she'd just started picking it up—and that she also had her own fantasy team.

Now they knew Sophie was legit and slowly began accepting her into the informal culture of their office. She didn't adopt all aspects of the culture but realized the effort was probably worth it to break into the inner circle. She actually began to enjoy the fantasy team and keeping current on the stats, and the ultimate payoff was that it connected her with her colleagues and enabled work to happen much more effectively.

Action Steps

- List the issues and cultural dynamics that typically create head-winds in your organization. (If you're unsure, simply think about a few projects or initiatives that failed, and list the reasons why.)

- List the issues and cultural dynamics that typically enhance engagement and results in your organization. (If you're unsure, simply think about a few projects or initiatives that were extremely successful, and list the reasons why.)

- Imagine you are asked to mentor a new employee. What words of advice would you give her to help her navigate the culture—not just its surface culture, but its *deep* culture?

- Then list the steps you should take to better navigate your organization's culture. Don't assume you're already doing everything you can, because you're not.

CHAPTER 4
Understanding and Connecting with People

"100% of employees are people. 100% of customers are people. 100% of vendors, of ALL stakeholders... are people. If you don't understand people, you don't understand business."

—SIMON SINEK

areed was leading a new team at the financial institution where he was working but was struggling to connect with a few of his people. One of his teammates, Otto, was a nice enough guy but seemed a bit standoffish. He only spoke up in meetings when he had something really important to say or when he was called upon. When people from the team would go out to dinner together, Otto would inevitably decline their invitations. Fareed tried harder to get him to join them but was met with more declined invitations. It seemed that Otto felt like he was becoming Fareed's project, and began withdrawing.

Meanwhile, another teammate, Andie, seemed to be challenging Fareed's authority as a leader, and rarely let anything go without pushing back, sometimes rather strongly. Fareed, a congenial guy, just blew it off and tried his best to establish harmony with her. He wasn't sure how to interpret either of these situations. He wrote it off as being in the team formation stage of "storming" (from the famous "forming, storming, norming, performing" model), and that once people got to know each other, things would work themselves out. But things *didn't* work themselves out, and the flawed dynamic remained.

After going through training on personality differences, Fareed realized that these people were just wired differently than he was. His strategy of interacting with them in a one-size-fits-all model, based on what worked for his personality, wasn't effective, and it would never magically become effective. So instead of practicing insanity by doing the same thing over and over again and expecting a different result, he shifted his approach to working with their personalities using what I like to call the Savvy Rule.

What is the Savvy Rule? It's simple:

Be keenly aware and adjust to enhance engagement, reduce headwinds, and optimize for results.

People are key to the success of any organization; that's why so many claim "People are our number one asset." That's actually true, but unfortunately, that phrase is often used to pay lip service to the concept of how important people are to an effective business. So, what about taking it seriously? If people *are* the number one asset of an organization, then it makes sense to learn how to work better with various types of people. Leaders who can read people are able to make adjustments to work better with them.

In a nutshell, the definition of Emotional Intelligence, or EQ comes down to people awareness, and then adjusting to be more effective. Research has revealed that leaders who have high emotional intelligence are much more effective in their leadership.[4]

At the heart of EQ is awareness of self and others. Often people don't spend the extra time to understand others before trying to lead them, simply because they're so busy. They mistakenly assume that other people are wired pretty much as they are, as in Fareed's example.

One of the most obvious places you see this at play is during a keynote speech at a conference. It's easy to spot a speaker who's just delivered a canned speech. Their connection with the audience is diminished because they haven't analyzed and adjusted for their audience. They've violated Rule Number One of public speaking: know your audience. Then there are the speakers who do the extra diligence needed to know their audience and adjust for them. This creates a charismatic dynamic that engages the audience and makes them feel special, resulting in a successful presentation.

At a recent leadership development conference in Chicago, a VP of Business Development at an international retail chain was speaking. From the beginning, he acknowledged what many in the audience were thinking, "Why did they choose a VP of Business Development to speak to an HR/Learning and Development audience?" He spoke directly to that question, then shared why he saw leadership development as such an integral part of their international business development strategy.

He blew us all away. He knew his audience and made the adjustments necessary to make his talk extremely relevant to us.

While this may seem like common sense, it was a new insight for Fareed, because his decision that he should lead others as if they had the same personality he had was a subconscious one. This was interesting, because Fareed had three children and was aware that he parented them differently depending on their unique personalities—but he didn't apply the same lesson at work until he had the insight of adjusting his leadership approach for different people's personalities.

Five Factors of Personality

As we learned in Chapter 3, *we see what we know*. The same thing applies to being able to read people. If we know the basic personality factors, we can see them in our everyday lives. Nowadays, there as many personality theories as there are days in the year (some of them very popular and surprisingly low on statistical validity), but there's one, most often used in research psychology, called the Five-Factor Model. The running joke is that if you take a bunch of psychologists, lock them in a room, and ask them to agree on a way to understand personality, the

Five-Factor Model is what they would all agree to.[5]

The acronym OCEAN helps make the five factors easier to remember:

- **Openness:** Creative vs. Conventional

- **Conscientiousness:** Organized vs. Spontaneous

- **Extraversion:** Outgoing vs. Reserved

- **Agreeableness:** Empathetic vs. Challenging

- **Neuroticism:** Nervous vs. Calm

Once you know these personality constructs, it's easier to see them. Everyone's personality can be assessed on each of the five factors, on a scale of high to low. While people may be somewhere in the middle on many of the five factors, when you think about them, you can often identify one or two factors that are more extreme in that person. Those are the factors that can make the most difference when you adjust for them.[6]

Thinking back to the examples at the beginning of this chapter, it becomes more evident that Otto was probably low on the extraversion scale. It wasn't that he was trying to be standoffish or rude, but that he had to steward his energy in a different way because of his lower level of extroversion. He might prefer a night out with just one friend, instead of several; otherwise he would feel drained, whereas Fareed is high on the extraversion scale and actually gets more energy from group get-togethers. Once he understood that Otto's personality was wired for low extraversion, Fareed started to engage him in a different way, applying less pressure to join in the extracurricular activities, proposing more one-on-one time instead. This created a stronger connection between Fareed and Otto, because Fareed was adjusting his approach based on Otto's personality rather than Fareed's.

Thinking back to Andie, she was clearly low on the agreeableness scale, so she was predisposed to disagree and push back, sometimes in a rather hard way. In his mind, Fareed had labeled her as a "jerk". But once he understood that her personality was low on the agreeableness scale, it changed how he viewed her. It was too easy to write her off as a difficult person. He decided to take it upon himself to change how he interacted with her. He focused on the bottom line and results in a way that might have felt harsh to others, but made a strong connection with her.

With both examples, Fareed was able to identify the parts of their personalities that were primary drivers. Once he was aware of each person's unique OCEAN Personality, he made adjustments to better connect with them. To Otto and Andie, this felt like someone finally "got them" and was speaking their personality language, just as Sophie in Chapter 3 did when she learned sports stats to better connect with her colleagues in a sports focused culture.

It's helpful to understand some general ways that you can adjust for someone based on their OCEAN Personality. Everyone is unique, so these won't work for everyone, but they are meant to spark some ideas for adjustments.

- *High Openness:* Focus on innovative ways to do things.
- *Low Openness:* Emphasize traditional ways of doing things.

- *High Conscientiousness:* Focus on structure.
- *Low Conscientiousness:* Focus on flexibility.

- *High Extraversion:* Increase your energy level.
- *Low Extraversion:* Focus more on 1-on-1 situations.

- *High Agreeableness:* Focus on how it will benefit others.
- *Low Agreeableness:* Focus on business logic and facts.

- *High Neuroticism:* Provide extra empathy to keep them calm.
- *Low Neuroticism:* Maintain a calm demeanor.

It's also important to help others make adjustments to be more effective. For example, you may need to ask someone who is high on agreeableness to negotiate harder to strike a better deal. You may need to ask someone who is low on

> conscientiousness to increase their attention to details and follow through for a particular project or situation. Or you may need to ask someone who is low on extraversion to go the extra mile and meet in-person with a client to close an important deal. Remember, you aren't asking them to change their personality, rather you are asking them to be agile in how they approach the particular task or situation to improve their effectiveness.

Using the Savvy Rule goes beyond the OCEAN Five Factors; it also extends into understanding questions, such as:

- What triggers headwinds (resistance) with them?

- What creates engagement with them?

- How do they typically make decisions?

- What are their goals?

- What drives them?

Knowing the answers to these questions enables you to better apply the Savvy Rule. Savvy Leaders do the extra work to know their audience before they get into a challenging situation, so they can maximize their chances to enhance engagement, reduce headwinds, and optimize for results, effectively leading the audience across the engagement J-Curve instead of the compliance curve or headwinds curve.

Sounds smart, right? So don't just agree. Take action! To become a better leader literally overnight, simply analyze their personality on the five factors and answer the above five questions for each of your employees. Once you do, you'll have a clear road map for best engaging each of them. Unlike the average manager, you won't try to lead using a one-size-fits-all approach. You'll treat each employee as an individual, better understanding how to help them do their best work and how to truly engage them... and you will have taken an important step on your personal journey to Savvy Leadership.

As you think about the **people awareness** aspect of leadership and the link to results, it's helpful to assess where each person is on a stakeholder analysis. This is most easily done by using a stakeholder four-box grid like the one below.

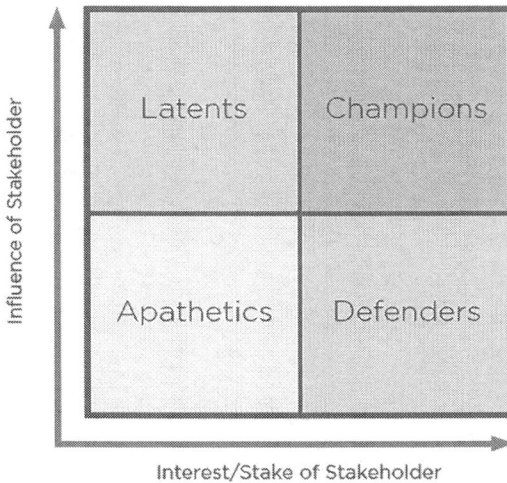

- An **Apathetic** is someone who has little interest in what you're trying to accomplish and lacks the influence to help make it happen anyway.

- A **Latent** is someone who also has little interest in what you're trying to accomplish, but *does* have the influence to help make it happen. They have potential, but it needs to be activated if they are to help accomplish your desired result. Later in the book, we'll talk more about how to effectively influence someone to activate their latent potential to support your goals.

- A **Defender** is someone who has keen interest in what you're trying to accomplish, but unfortunately doesn't have much influence to help make it happen. These people can be great groundswell supporters.

- A **Champion** is someone who has both keen interest in what you're trying to accomplish, and the influence to help make it happen. Clearly, these are great people to have on board and to collaborate with.

But there's another category hidden in the grid that you have to be aware of:

- **Defeaters** can occupy the same quadrant as the Champions. They have interest and influence, but they're only interested in defeating your desired result, so they use their influence to oppose it.

When considering the journey along the J-Curve from where you are now to where you want to be, it's key to think through where various people fit on a stakeholder quadrant. When you do that, you may realize that you have many people in the Latent or Apathetic quadrants and very few in the Defender or Champion quadrants, in which case you have your work cut out for you. That doesn't mean you can't make it happen; it just means that you'll need to work to activate some of the people in the Latent quadrant in order to gain more support. You will also want to ensure that the few Champions and/or Defenders you do have are on board to collaborate with you.

Again, knowing the personalities of the people in the quadrant will help you connect with them and work with them to make your desired result a reality. It's an efficiency, effectiveness, and engagement tool to help you be a Savvy Leader who knows how to work with people who are at different places of readiness to drive results.

People Awareness Conclusion

Leaders who pay lip-service to the importance of their people often pay the price with low performance and resentment. Savvy Leaders are keenly aware not only of the importance of knowing their people, but also of the importance of adjusting to other personalities, instead of waiting for a miracle to occur where everyone adjusts to them. It's the leader's responsibility to adjust and set the dynamic of the relationship with each person.

Savvy Leaders are able to check their egos at the door in order to be in service to what works for others. This doesn't mean that you're not true to who you are; it simply means you're wisely flexible. Sometimes there's a limit to how much adjusting will benefit you, and that's where other options need to be considered in order to get the dynamic to a place where it works. We'll come back to that later in this book.

Action Steps

- Apply the Savvy Rule to your workplace: answer the five questions for each of your direct reports as well as key stakeholders. (And don't forget to include your boss.)

- List the people you most frequently work with, then estimate their OCEAN Personalities.

- Consider some areas where you're holding too tightly onto your own style, to the point that it's impacting your ability to improve interpersonal dynamics with others. Then list changes you should make, starting tomorrow.

- Finally, think about your team and identify ways you can you increase your personal flexibility in order to improve the interpersonal dynamics on that team. (Remember: while you can't always change others, you can always change yourself.)

SECTION
TWO

ENHANCING
ENGAGEMENT

- Relational Engagement

- Motivational Engagement

CHAPTER 5
Relational Engagement

> "Train people well enough so they can leave.
> Treat them well enough so they don't want to."
>
> —SIR RICHARD BRANSON,
> ENGLISH BUSINESS MAGNATE, INVESTOR, AND PHILANTHROPIST

Engagement activates high performance. If you've ever been part of team with a high engagement level, then you know what it feels like. Unfortunately, the engagement levels of employees within the U.S. have stubbornly hovered around 70 percent disengaged, a fact supported by numerous annual studies and polls, including several by Gallup.[7] Many organizations have come to rely heavily on surveys to build their awareness of the engagement levels of people at their organizations, and this has provided some insight. Perhaps as a result, in recent years, full engagement has inched slightly upward.

Unfortunately, this insight hasn't been enough to create significant change. In fact, surveys not followed by significant changes can create unnecessary headwinds and stifle engagement, because it then seems that leaders either don't care enough to make any changes, or are too incompetent to know how. Either way, it sends a bad message. This creates a huge missed opportunity, because teams with high levels of engagement have lower turnover rates, more commitment, more effort, better attitudes, and stronger performance. Think of it this way: settling for low engagement is like leaving big bags of money on the table. The key question, then, becomes, *how do you activate greater levels of engagement with the people you work with?*

We defined employee engagement in Chapter 2 as:

---

the level of commitment and motivation to work hard and give discretionary effort.

Commitment is both psychological and emotional. The psychological part stems from how people process the leadership dynamic. It includes things such as the level of trust that's been developed, belief in the leader's competence, the internal dialogue, and assumptions of intent about the leader, all of which factor into a person's commitment level and results in their personal choice to give or withhold discretionary effort.

The emotional aspect of commitment has to do with how the person feels about the leader. Does the team member admire them, or feel inspired by them? Or does the team member feel misunderstood, threatened, or even just irrelevant or ignored by them? All of this feeds into the engagement equation of the team member, which affects their private vote to expend or withhold their discretionary efforts.

As also mentioned in Chapter 2, a costly mistake that many leaders make when they sense low levels of engagement (i.e., the compliance J-Curve) is that they double-down on stronger command-and-control styles of leadership, which makes things worse (see the headwinds J-Curve) and hastens a scenario where people start shopping their resumes around. A situation where there's a low level of engagement, and the leader tries to force people into volunteering their discretionary effort is like the Chinese finger trap: the more force you use, the more stuck you become. The Pirate Incentive doesn't work, and neither does the old-fashioned one I saw on a sign in a convenience store one day, "New Incentive Plan: Work or Get Fired."

Make no mistake, any employee who's been in his or her job more than a month knows *exactly* how much work they have to do to achieve the minimum required to keep their jobs. But here's the thing—every single day, each worker has the power of personal choice about whether or not to volunteer extra effort at work. As a leader, how you lead every day, in good times and bad, greatly impacts that choice.

To repeat a recurring theme, the Savvy Leader knows that **how you lead matters**.

Most leaders understand the benefits of developing a highly engaged team, but they don't know *how* to do it. The key is to lead in a way that activates the engagement J-Curve we looked at in Chapter 2. It's not just one thing that does this, but a number of factors working together to drive the engagement dynamic—just like the 96 small motors moving the massive 22-million-pound roof of Safeco Field. The good news is that there's potential all around us; it just takes a modest degree of leadership savvy to know how to activate it. The two main pathways to enhancing engagement are **relational** and **motivational**.

Relational Engagement

Relational engagement is the degree to which the relationship between leader and follower enhances engagement. Let's start with the worst-case scenario. Have you ever worked in an organization or on a team where there was low (or no) relational engagement? People don't care about each other, and loyalty is low. They clock in and out exactly when they're supposed to; no one arrives early or stays late because they aren't willing to put forth extra effort. Why? One common reason is because their leader hasn't invested in them relationally.

That's not to say that you have to become best friends or even friends with your team members in order to build relational engagement. But because we're all human beings, if there's a lack of authentic connection with the leader, this necessarily leads to lowered relational engagement levels. This may not be viewed as problematic when things are going well, but the problem becomes acute when difficult situations arise, and *that* is when relational engagement is most essential.

On the flipside, relational engagement can provide the extra juice to make seemingly impossible things happen. A shining example is Miguel, a regional manager at a retail company I met at a conference where I was speaking. He was the "golden boy" of his group, and I soon found out why. Everyone who worked with him loved him, and his was the top-performing team in the company. This data point ruffled the feathers of many who had a more traditional command-and-control style of leadership because they felt that his was a "soft" style of leadership. In fact, it was—but obviously, "soft" doesn't necessarily mean "ineffective." As part of my work with them, I did a ride-along as he visited stores. It was evident when he walked into each store that he was a welcome sight, as opposed to other leaders, who caused employees to take on a deer-in-the-headlights look when they appeared.

Miguel spent time—not a lot, but a few minutes—intentionally connecting with each person prior to transitioning into talking about the business. It was evident that the employees felt valued and respected through this approach. The consistency in his approach set a foundation where people felt more freedom to speak up, which gave Miguel the opportunity to fine-tune things and maintain a high-performance environment.

The degree of relational engagement that Miguel developed with his team was also key when he had to make changes. Instead of facing the headwinds curve, he was able to lead his teams through the changes on the engagement curve of stronger commitment and effort. This was a stark contrast to the other leaders in the organization. At the end of the conference, Miguel received the MVP Award—and it was also announced that he was being promoted to Regional Vice-President, to which there was a standing ovation.

What is it that people like Miguel do differently to build high levels of relational engagement? The most important thing is that he connected with his employees through the micro-moments of leadership. There's a saying that's particularly true in higher relational cultures:

"Contact before content." In other words, before diving into the business content, make contact with the other person; connect with them. This will look different depending on whom you're working with. Most people want some connection, and it's the exception—*not* the rule—that some view it as unnecessary. So again, knowing your audience can help you adjust to become better at connecting in a way that builds stronger relational engagement.

The Three Ways to Develop Relational Engagement

There are three main routes to developing stronger relational engagement: **listening**, **empathy**, and **the Magic Ratio**. Genuine, active listening is the most common way to connect with people, even in time-pressed situations. A relevant example comes from a study that was conducted to determine the reasons why patients chose not to sue their surgeons when they made mistakes. What they found was that the surgeons who had spent extra time listening to their patients were much less likely to get sued. We know that physicians are hard-pressed for time (just as most people are in the modern workplace), so the researchers focused on how much listening time, on average, made the tipping point difference. Their discovery was astonishing; it took *just three extra minutes* of active listening to build a connection with a patient to the point where the patient was much more likely to forgive rather than punish the surgeon for mistakes.[8]

Think about how that applies to leadership in the trenches. Everyone is busy, but recall a time when a leader stopped by to say hello and showed genuine interest in you. People remember such things, and that can make all the difference in activating relational engagement. It may be one of the most important things a leader can do; and yet, it's so easy to neglect, because we prioritize the tyranny of the urgent over the important, and/or we fear that we will be perceived as "soft" instead of a hard-driver if we actually show interest in our teammates.

I used the word "teammates" deliberately here. As the leader, you're also a member of the team, so the other team members are in fact your teammates. Make them feel this deep down, and they're more likely to engage.

Empathy, the ability to make people feel seen and understood, is another powerful way to build relational engagement. It's the number one tool of psychotherapists, and any leader who doesn't use it undermines their own effectiveness. Empathy has numerous benefits, including, but not limited to:

- Improving understanding

- Building trust

- Crafting a sense of safety

- Creating resonance

- Reducing defensiveness

Now, think about that last one. When people get into conflicts, those conflicts are often made worse by a lack of empathy. When empathy is provided in a conflict, it tends to de-escalate situations, and can actually help shift the dynamic to collaborative problem solving. One of the most powerful ways of expressing empathy is through the phrase, "I hear where you're coming from. It sounds like _____ is important to you."

One balancing note on empathy: many resist providing empathy because they equate it with agreement. For example, consider a salesperson who's complaining about the lack of responsiveness of a key client. Many leaders would argue with the salesperson rather than display empathy because they're afraid it will be perceived as "letting them off the hook." But understanding and agreeing aren't the same thing. An alternative way to lead in this situation is to have "thick-skinned empathy." That is, provide the empathy so they feel heard and understood, then move into coaching them to collaboratively resolve the problem. Without the empathy aspect, they're likely to think you don't understand and aren't willing to help collaboratively, which will likely lead to a lowering of performance and of relational engagement.

The Magic Ratio is the third way to develop relational engagement. This is a rule based on research originally done on healthy marriages. The Gottman Institute in Seattle studies the components of healthy marriages by inviting couples to their "love lab," where they study their interactions. Given all of the data they've accumulated over the years, they can observe a couple for just 15 minutes and, with 94 percent accuracy, predict whether or not the couple will get divorced. A major component they look for is the ratio of positive to negative interactions. The Magic Ratio that signifies a healthy relationship is at least 5:1—that is, five positive interactions for each negative one.[9]

There's almost certainly a magic ratio in the workplace as well. What exactly that ratio is remains up for debate. It's likely not as high as the ratio for healthy marriages, but likely higher than what most people tend to give or receive through the course of a work day. Some suggest a ratio of 3:1. This ratio provides a healthy balance of positive and realistic negative energy in work relationships.

For most leaders, this ratio is a wake-up call to be more proactive, to ensure they're interacting with their teams in a way that builds relational engagement. I've even seen leaders put reminders on their smartphones or smart watches to get them into the habit of providing more routine positive interactions, even if it's just small compliments. It works surprisingly well.

Developing strong relational engagement not only makes the good times better, but it's also extremely valuable when things are tough. There's a networking book titled *Dig Your Well Before You're Thirsty* by Harvey McKay. In it, McKay refers to the need to build up your professional network ("dig your well") before you need it ("before you're thirsty"). The same thing is true with building relational engagement. If you need to lead your team across a gap to a new result, which is what leaders are doing by definition every day, you'll improve your odds of success if you've done the intentional, proactive work of developing strong relational engagement with your team before needing to lean on it.

Savvy Leaders also build relational engagement by answering the unasked question.

People often ask a different question than the one they really want you to answer. Maybe they're hesitant. Maybe they're insecure. One employee might ask whether you think he should take a few business classes; what he really wants to know is whether you see him as able to grow in your organization. He hopes you'll say you do, and hopes you'll share the reasons why. Your wife might ask if you thought the guy at the party was flirting with her; what she really wants to know is if you still think she's flirt-worthy and whether you still find her attractive. She hopes you'll say you do, and she'll love when you share the reasons why.

Behind many questions is an unasked question. Pay attention so you can answer that question, too, because that is the answer the other person doesn't just want, but *needs*. When you answer that question, you connect on a much deeper level with that employee and show a level of empathy few leaders display.

Another way to show empathy is what we talked about first: listen better. Why don't more leaders actively listen to what their employees have to say? For one thing, it's easy to assume you have all the answers when you're in charge. Listening is easy. Ask questions. Maintain eye contact. Smile. Frown. Nod. Respond—not so much verbally, but non-verbally. That's all it takes to show other people that they are important.

Then, when you *do* speak, don't offer advice unless you're asked. Listening shows you care a lot more than offering advice does, because when you offer advice, in most cases, you make the conversation about yourself and not the other person. (Think about it. If you say, "Here is what I would do..." who is that really about—you, or the person you're speaking to?)

Savvy Leaders often define "important" as what matters to the other person and not to themselves.

If you have a new team, you may not have the luxury of months or years of developing relational engagement. But remember, it doesn't have to take a lot of time to develop relational engagement. With surgeons, it only took a few moments of active listening to build enough relational engagement to create a dynamic of collaboration rather than one of compliance or resistant headwinds. Theodore Roosevelt summed it up well, "People won't care what you have to say until they know how much you care."

Action Steps

- Consider your standard default when it comes to leadership. (Be honest.) How does it impact relational engagement?

- Think about several times or situations when your teams have been at their most productive. What role did engagement have on their performance? List the reasons why engagement was so high.

- Think about leaders you have worked for who made you feel motivated, engaged, and committed. Their words and actions made you feel that way. What can you borrow from their example?

- Now determine the steps you can take to lift and maintain employee engagement at those levels—and commit to turning those steps into actions.

CHAPTER 6
Motivational Engagement

"Never doubt that a small group of thoughtful, committed citizens can change the world; indeed, it's the only thing that ever has."

—MARGARET MEAD,
AMERICAN ANTHROPOLOGIST

J ake was a sales director at a medium-sized manufacturing company. During the annual sales strategy meeting led by the company executives, it was promised with great fanfare that whoever accomplished the sales goal using the new strategy would receive a trip to the Bahamas. Jake, along with many of his colleagues, later confessed that while they wouldn't say no to a free vacation, it wasn't the big motivator that their leaders thought it was.

What they were craving was to be better motivated as *people*; not just for more money or things, but for more of the intangibles. In fact, a number of them also admitted that they were actively looking for a different place to work—a place where they could make a similar amount of money, but where the leadership was more appreciative of their employees.

Motivational engagement is the other half of the "enhancing engagement" formula. It's most effective when built on a solid base of relational engagement because it thrives on trust. Motivational engagement aligns with how people are truly wired, deepening their psychological and emotional commitment, thus helping activate the choice to contribute discretionary effort to their work.

Our understanding of motivation has undergone rapid evolution over the past 20 years. Even so, there remain two main categories of motivation: **extrinsic** and **intrinsic**. Extrinsic motivation is motivation that comes from outside an individual, like a reward or a bonus, or even your salary. When companies receive poor engagement survey results, they often try to buy their way into better engagement rates by offering extra benefits (extrinsic motivations). More often than not, they're surprised and disappointed to see a poor ROI on those motivators, as was the case with Jake and his colleagues.

But if extrinsic motivation isn't very effective beyond a specific baseline, what is? Intrinsic motivation, which is internal: things like your level of enjoyment, curiosity, sense of empowerment, challenge, or mission. Intrinsic motivation is powerful and sustainable. Even better, it's free, although you do have to invest some time and energy to activate it. But that's all part of the job. Savvy Leaders understand that after building a foundation of relational engagement, ensuring that a healthy baseline of extrinsic motivation is in place, the next area to focus on is intrinsic motivation, in order to activate the full power of motivational engagement.

Intrinsic motivation is primarily activated by three things: Purpose, Ego, and Development (**PED**).

Purpose

One of the top 20 most-viewed TED Talks is one by Simon Sinek entitled, "How Great Leaders Inspire Action." Any guesses about his answer? Don't worry, I won't keep you in suspense. It's **the power of "why."**[10] People are wired to want to know *why* they're doing what they're doing. They want to know that what they're laboring over has a greater purpose than just punching a clock for a paycheck (i.e., extrinsic motivation). In the new work culture, people realize they have more choices in their career paths, and we all want one that's meaningful and makes a difference. Many leaders can't seem to grasp this. Research by Levit and Licina reveals that while Millennials typically rank a job with greater purpose as more important than one with higher pay, their leaders often make the mistake of assuming the opposite—so they motivate their teammates the wrong way, which stifles motivational engagement.[11]

Researcher and author Adam Grant shares an example of how understanding the purpose of your job can increase your motivation and performance. There was a call center responsible for raising funds for a non-profit organization. Employees were compliant about doing their fundraising calls, but they were uninspiring on the phone. A Savvy Leader realized he needed to do something to activate intrinsic motivation, building their motivational engagement. He focused on helping them understand the purpose of what they were doing, simply by inviting people in to share their stories of how they, personally, had benefited from the non-profit the employees were raising funds for.

When they made the connection between what they were doing on the phone and the good that the non-profit was doing for its end users, the employees' fundraising performance spiked 171 percent—without them even being conscious of it. It wasn't some big, fancy program that motivated them; it was simply a matter of making a personal connection to the impact of their work. That helped them gain a greater sense of purpose, which then enhanced their engagement.[12]

Dennis worked in a run-and-gun book manufacturing plant. The goal wasn't to produce the highest quality product possible; the goal was to avoid customer complaints while maximizing productivity. Publicly, management might have disagreed with that goal, but since there's often a difference between what is said and what is expected, shop floor employees were well aware of the real expectations. Numbers mattered—a lot.

(Now, keep in mind that I don't disagree with striking a balance between quality and productivity. Commodity production, especially when price is the major competitive factor, requires meeting quality expectations while maximizing output and minimizing costs. Exceeding quality expectations is fine, as long as it doesn't slow you down or cost you more.)

In the mid-1980s, Dennis's plant expanded its printing and binding capabilities to include Bible and hymnal production. Convincing publishers they could reliably manufacture Bibles and hymn books wasn't easy for the sales team; one publisher even sent a Vice President to talk to everyone at the plant involved in producing their work. "You aren't running books," she told them. "You're running *Bibles*."

At first, Dennis assumed she was speaking from a religious perspective. Years later, he realized her statement carried a larger meaning. Her point was that a Bible can be more than just a book; it can also be a cherished gift, a source of comfort, or an heirloom passed on from one generation to the next. In short, a Bible can take on a meaning greater than the words it contains. Unlike a "regular" book, a Bible might be more than just a book to be read once and placed on a shelf; it could, over time—even if a page is never turned—become an item that takes on real significance in a person's or a family's life.

So can almost anything. What a business sells, no matter how transitory, may turn out to have a larger meaning. A restaurant doesn't just serve food; a restaurant may create a touchstone for a family's memories. A smartphone may not just store music and images, but could provide the soundtrack and photo album of a teenager's life. Clothing might be worn on the first day of school or on a first date.

The products and services you provide can, at times, make a lasting impact in a customer's life. Savvy Leaders help their employees understand how they provide customers with much more than a product or service. Maybe that "more" is better quality. Maybe it's better service. Maybe it's the recognition that most purchases have an objective and an emotional component, and that emotional component must be supported during and after the sales process.

Sharing the purpose of work is the default mode for Savvy Leaders. It shouldn't be left up to the individual worker to dig up or define meaning for the work they're doing. It's part of the leader's responsibility to define and share the meaning even in the small things; otherwise, you're devaluing the impact of motivational engagement. Savvy Leaders are proactive about this when making work assignments, readily providing the work's purpose and explaining how each person advances the goals of the entire organization.

Ego

The ego part of intrinsic motivation is what makes people feel good about themselves. It's built up from three main components: **Dignity and Respect**, **Belonging**, and **Empowerment**. People want to be to be treated with dignity and respect. They also want to feel like they belong, like they're part of the team. They want to be empowered, not micromanaged.

An interesting study was done to see what happens to engagement when coupled with various levels of respect. The researchers found a very close correlation between the degree of respect and the level of engagement.

"Being respectful doesn't just benefit you, though; it benefits everyone around you. In a study of nearly 20,000 employees around the world (conducted with HBR), I found that when it comes to garnering commitment and engagement from employees, there's one thing that leaders need to demonstrate: respect. No other leadership behavior had a bigger effect on employees across the outcomes we measured. Being treated with respect was more important to employees than recognition and appreciation, communicating an inspiring vision, providing useful feedback—or even opportunities for learning, growth, and development."

—CHRISTINE PORATH IN HARVARD BUSINESS REVIEW[13]

The respect/engagement connection was exhibited in the style of Raj, a regional director of operations for a logistics company. The people on his team, even when challenged, felt there was a line of respect and dignity that he honored. That enabled them to bring their tough challenges to the table because they would be met with a respectful tone—which was unlike the style of their preceding leader. Previously, workers had been reluctant to bring up issues, because of the lack of respect and dignity. Because they were able to work through tough challenges with Raj, rather than avoid them, they gained a greater sense of accomplishment and ownership, which helped to activate their motivational engagement.

The second component of Ego is belonging. Time to step into the WABAC machine. Remember wanting to be part of a group as a kid, but not quite fitting in—or perhaps even being rejected? Most people I know can relate to this, and unfortunately, many of them also confess that it didn't stop when they became adults; it's still at play at work. There are a few among them, though, who rave about their workplaces. One of the things they invariably mention is that they have a strong team dynamic where people have each other's backs.

The dynamics of belonging can be challenging to create in the modern workplace because there are so many short-term assignments and free agents. A colleague of mine is a consultant, and he jokes about being "unemployable" because he enjoys the freedom of being an external specialist. However, he's also confessed to me that he's often very lonely as a result. So he intentionally chooses client work where he's welcomed as part of the team, and where there's a sense of camaraderie built by overcoming challenges together (rather than bonding over complaints of poor leadership). This creates a sense of belonging to which he brings his best efforts... and he's even willing to charge less!

I've witnessed many situations where people have left their positions because they didn't share a sense of belonging with their team. I've also seen cases where there was a strong sense of belonging which kept people with the team over the long haul, even when other factors were less than ideal. Belonging is a tipping point that can activate motivational engagement—or deactivate it.

The third component here is empowerment. Part of what drives great employees to become free agents/external consultants is that they've had bad experiences working for leaders who micromanaged them. The image of a caged animal at the zoo comes to mind in such situations. If employees are expected to connect effectively to the purpose of their work, then they need to be empowered to do it. Micromanagement only leads to people feeling small.

With clarity of purpose and responsibility, empowerment is a powerful builder of motivational engagement.

Development

People have an innate desire to grow and make things happen. But often, they get pigeonholed into a particular role, which leads to a flat learning curve and little growth. For a leader, it might be tempting to do this for simplicity's sake, but when applied as a default, it inevitably leads to a decline in engagement. I've even encountered some leaders who purposefully *don't* develop their team members because they don't want them to become more competent and leave the team. This mentality comes from a place of scarcity and doesn't attract, create, or retain engaged employees.

Living in Seattle, I've been watching how Pete Carroll coaches the Seattle Seahawks football team. The core of his coaching philosophy is developing talent rather than just acquiring it. This is evident in a number of ways. He recruits strong players and develops them into great players. He notices their natural strengths and doesn't hesitate to move people from their traditional roles into different positions before developing them to excel. The thing that most stood out for me was when he was asked how he felt about losing some of his best assistant coaches when they were recruited to become head coaches at other NFL teams. He said, "That's great!" He took it as a sign that his program was viewed as a place where people's talents are developed to excellence. That made it even more attractive for people to want to coach and play for him, even though his team is located in the cloudy, rainy corner of the country. Some players were even willing to take a "hometown" discount to stay and play for him for less money than they could have made elsewhere.

A helpful way to view the development part of motivational engagement is the concept of "flow" developed by Mihály Csíkszentmihályi. The essence of his theory is that people feel most motivated when they're "in the zone" of facing challenges that develop their competence. If they have an abundance of competence but not enough challenge, they get bored. If they have an abundance of challenge but are significantly lacking competence, they get overwhelmed. In both cases, performance and motivation take a hit. But if you can match a person or team to a challenge that reasonably stretches their competence, you'll be setting them up for the zone of high engagement and performance.[14]

Flow[6]

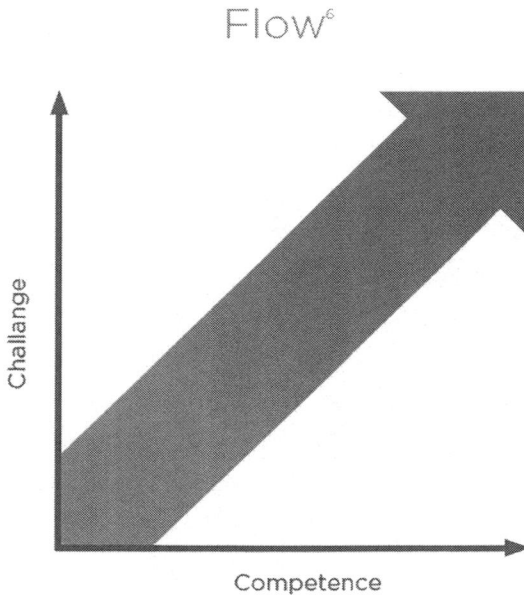

Challenge (y-axis) / Competence (x-axis)

So, how do you find out where someone is on this scale? Just show the graph to them and ask them, and then do some strategic planning. It's a simple but powerful development conversation that should be happening at least monthly throughout the year. If you find yourself doing it less often—or worse, not doing it at all—push yourself to start scheduling these meetings and associated discussions on a regular basis. By doing so, you'll be indicating that you care about your team member's development and that you take it seriously.

Effective leaders also set clear expectations, so communicate exactly what you want that worker to accomplish—and make sure they understand by asking them questions and keep repeating the process until they understand. The typical team member will catch on pretty quickly, but be patient if someone has to ask a lot of questions before they get it down solidly in their minds. The more internalized the task, the more likely they will be able to handle it automatically.

A sense of accomplishment can be a big motivator for people, so be intentional about noticing and calling it out when goals are met. Likewise, when people fall short, respectfully challenge and empower them to do better.

Summary

Savvy Leaders consistently develop the motivational engagement of their teams by doing the little things that make a difference when it comes to the personal choice of contributing discretionary efforts or not. It doesn't take extra money; it just takes extra effort and discipline to activate it.

Action Steps

- Take a look at your personal motivational style: is it weighted more heavily toward extrinsic or intrinsic motivation?

- List ways you can shift your current balance more in your favor (and ways you can start to "manage up" to help your boss support your personal motivation preference.)

- Then consider the Savvy Rules answers you listed for each employee in Chapter 4 and list steps you can take to skew that balance towards inspiring intrinsic motivation among each of your direct reports.

- Finally, list ways you can start to influence your organization's culture so that its overall motivational style will maximize productivity. Remember, Savvy Leaders seek to make *everyone* better.

SECTION
THREE

REDUCING
HEADWINDS

- Power

- Influence

CHAPTER 7
Power

> "Nearly all men can stand adversity,
> but if you want to test a man's character, give him power."
>
> —ABRAHAM LINCOLN,
> 16TH PRESIDENT OF THE UNITED STATES

"*They call it work for a reason.*"

Solomon is a hard-working employee at a farming equipment supply company in Iowa. He comes to work every day on time, with a genuine interest in helping the customers who walk through the door. His role is in customer support, so when the customer has a problem, Solomon is the one they turn to. The customer support team recently got a new team leader named Derrick, who was promoted from the sales team. Derrick is a highly-motivated self-starter. As he took the reins of the customer support team, he made it clear who was in charge. He was used to being in a hyper-competitive, individual contributor role, and that was how he led the team. There was little collaboration, relationship, or motivation.

Before long, things started turning sour. Solomon was "nominated" by his team to tell Derrick how the rest of the team felt. Solomon wasn't thrilled about drawing the short straw and having to be the one to talk with Derrick, but when he considered the impact of doing nothing, he mustered the courage to do it. Derrick replied, "You know what? The

CST is so soft! You guys need to get a backbone. Customer support is in existence because of customer problems, and if you can't deal with problems, then maybe this isn't the right job for you. You know, they call it work for a reason!" Solomon was stunned, and needless to say, felt like his work had just gotten a whole lot harder—not because of the customers, but because of the leadership dynamic of his new leader.

There will always be difficulty in the workplace; there's no getting around that. But how a leader leads through difficulty makes a big difference in how people perceive it and respond. Unfortunately, out of either fear, ignorance, or both, leaders often make it even worse. The extra, unnecessary headwinds they create are perceived as incompetent or uncaring leadership, and people feel the burn of the extra toil and burden. It creates the headwinds J-Curve we talked about in Chapter 2, where there's a deeper downside and people become demotivated and disengaged, capping performance with an artificially low ceiling. This is the other part of why engagement rates stay so stubbornly low: not only are leaders typically poor at enhancing engagement, they also often make things worse due to a lack of savvy.

The interesting thing here is that you can have two different leaders in the same circumstances who get entirely different results. One who leads their team through the difficulty via the engagement curve gets good results, and the other, who leads on the headwinds curve, ends up with underwhelming results and a burned-out team. Headwinds are most often caused by mismatches of power and influence. While a Savvy Leader using power and influence can produce outstanding results, both factors can quickly become a major source of headwinds.

Five Types of Power

Power is the ability to make things happen. French and Raven[15] narrowed down the types of power to five bases:

> **Legitimate Power** is power provided through hierarchy. The CEO of a company has plenty of Legitimate Power to make changes in

the organization, whereas an intern has very little.

Reward Power is the power to provide rewards. A sales director has the power to give rewards to people who meet their quotas.

Coercive Power is the power to punish, pressure, or make uncomfortable. A leader has the Coercive Power to fire people if they don't comply with a directive.

Expert Power comes from being viewed as competent. An external consultant who is brought in often has high Expert Power because of their expertise at navigating similar problems for others.

Referent Power stems from being likable, respected, or admired. Celebrities are often used to endorse products because of their Referent Power.

The five types of power can be grouped together into two categories, **Positional** and **Personal**. Positional types of power stem from one's position in an organization. Personal power stems from who the person is, regardless of their position in a hierarchy. Positional Power includes Legitimate, Reward, and Coercive Power. Expert and Referent Power are types of Personal Power.

Note that someone can have Reward or Coercive Power *without* the authority of being the official leader. For example, someone could offer to do someone else a favor, like letting them use their weekend cabin or getting them tickets to a ball game, to obtain a concession from them. This variety of Reward Power is often used in sales to entice the buyer (often to make up for a lack of Expert or Referent Power). Be careful here. Reward Power can easily tip into the kind of unethical behavior that shows up in the headlines as corruption.

Coercive Power can also be used without authority, and may also come close to or cross the line into unethical behavior, such as blackmail or withholding of effort. One example of coercive power being used in the workplace is the classic work slowdown. For example, at airlines, if the unions are struggling to get a new contract, the pilot and/or crew will often find minor reasons to delay the flight in order to "put the hurt" on management to make a deal on the contract before it damages the airline's reputation and stock price too much. If you see an airline suddenly struggle with their on-time departure statistics, it's often a result of the union employees using Coercive Power in negotiations.

Now it gets interesting. Let's see which curve each type of power tends to lead to.

- **Legitimate Power** leads to the compliance curve.

- **Reward Power** leads to the compliance curve.

- **Coercive Power** leads to the headwinds curve.

- **Expert Power** leads to the engagement curve.

- **Referent Power** leads to the engagement curve.[16]

Positional	Personal
Legitimate Compliance	Expert Engagement
Coercive Headwinds	Referent Engagement
Reward Compliance	

Savvy Leaders understand that their default mode should be the Personal types of power (Expert and Referent). They proactively and continually develop their expertise and strive to build relationships and behave in ways that strengthen their reputation. The more Personal Power they develop, the less Positional Power they have to use, and the higher the likelihood that they will drive the engagement curve. Those who view Personal Power as soft, and are more reliant on the power of their positions, have a difficult time creating a dynamic any better than the compliance curve. Unfortunately, people soon tire of their power trips and view the dynamic as one full of headwinds.

All that said, it's not so black-and-white as to say "only use Personal Power." There are times when a Savvy Leader should use more Positional Power. For example, when an employee is breaking the rules, this would be a time to use Coercive Power, so they know that if the behavior doesn't change, they will experience consequences.

Kira, a leader at a client company, was leading a meeting with her team. The discussion went around and around. The minutes were ticking away, and people had other stuff they needed to tend to, but it seemed like this meeting was getting stuck in the quicksand of consensus. Everyone was sticking to their own ideas, and no one was willing to bend. Finally, Kira stepped in and said, "This has been a very helpful discussion, but as much as I wish we could all agree, it doesn't look like we will—and someone's got to make the final call. In this case, as the team leader, that's me." And she announced what they were going to do. She made an appropriate use of her Legitimate Power. She didn't do it with a heavy hand, but rather in an assertive yet respectful way where people may have still disagreed, but were willing to climb on board and go with it.

Knowing the different types of power and the dynamics they create helps Savvy Leaders make a conscious choice about which ones they'll use and when they'll use them. Short-term and long-term effects and tradeoffs should be considered as you choose what type of power to lead from. Knowing about the power types also enables you to be savvy about what types of power are being used on you.

Power Tips

Each type of power can be used well or poorly. As a practical application, let's examine how to use each type of power well. We'll call these **Power Tips**.

Legitimate Power

- Make a clear and respectful request.

- Explain the rationale.

- Don't overstep your authority.

- Be assertive without enjoying a "power trip."

Reward Power

- Align rewards with the person's desires (using the Savvy Rule).

- Focus on intrinsic rewards.

- Be clear about the criteria for the reward, and don't move the target.

- Remove red tape to accomplish the reward.

Coercive Power

- Apply consistency and fairness for consequences.

- Be respectful and grounded (don't let it get overheated with emotions).

- Consider this the option of last resort, to be used sparingly and intentionally (not as a default).

Expert Power

- Don't exaggerate or be arrogant.

- Really know your stuff, and be open to learning more.

- Explain your rationale.

- Add value versus proving smarts.

Referent Power

- Celebrate small wins and give praise frequently.

- Earn trust, model accountability and enhance engagement.

- Be the best you that you can be.

- Be confident, caring, and authentic.

- Tend towards optimism and positivity.

- Stand up for respect and dignity.

When a Savvy Leader uses power in a proactive and thoughtful way that matches the situation, they're able to more frequently drive the engagement dynamic instead of unintentionally triggering the head-winds dynamic that makes work feel not just like work, but like toil.

Action Steps

- Think about which category of power you use most often: Personal or Positional. Then spend some time thinking about why you use that category of power. If you skew towards Positional, is it because you're inexperienced, or lack certain skills, or is that your organization's culture? Then determine steps you can take to feel more confident utilizing Personal Power more often.

- Then determine which is your default power base, and why you use it more than the other four types of power. Be honest and assess whether that power base is actually effective.

- Now determine the most effective use of power you have witnessed in your professional life. How would you classify that power?

- More importantly, list the steps you can take that will allow you to operate from an effective form of power—one that will drive results by inspiring and engaging your employees.

CHAPTER 8
Influence

"The greatest ability in business is
to get along with others and to influence their actions."

—JOHN HANCOCK,
AMERICAN MERCHANT, AND STATESMAN

Effective leadership has a great deal to do with how you influence others. Just like leadership power, depending on how you use it, your influence can engage people or create unnecessary headwinds to progress.

Take Marcus, for example. Marcus was recently hired as a director, straight from his role as an external consultant. He was given the assignment to lead the company's annual stockholder conference. It was a big deal, and he was thrilled to have it entrusted to him. As an external consultant, he already had a reputation for making things happen. While he'd had very little Positional Power, he used Expert and Referent Power to make things happen, which created both an engaged team and great results. But now he had the added bonus, and responsibility, of stewarding Positional Power. Because he was internal, he could use whatever power type he wanted.

Tired of being limited to Personal Power, Marcus decided he was going to use Positional Power a lot. This really showed up in the tactics he used to influence people. Just as with the bases of power, the types of influence tactics that leaders use can either reduce or worsen the headwinds of work. Marcus made them worse. It began with the way he interacted with the external vendors for the conference. He was not only very demanding of them, but demeaned them in a way that went far beyond hard bargaining. He didn't collaborate with them; instead, he just told them what to do and how they should do it. He kept them under his thumb. When they came up for air, he was sure to remind them that they needed to work even harder, because *he* was in charge based on the contract.

During the preparation for the conference, he started using the same tactics with people within his organization. For the most part, the vendors just dealt with it, but the people working with and for Marcus had soon had enough. Three of his people joined other teams the week after the conference was over. The vendor that Marcus had been pushing around announced that their prices were going up to the tune of 25 percent (essentially, a surcharge for dealing with Marcus). Within a month, enough feedback had been given to the VP about Marcus's way of "making things happen" that Marcus was relieved of his duties.

Marcus's defense was a common one from people who recklessly use their influence to achieve a short-term goal, "But look at the event, it was a big success!"

To which the VP replied, "Yes, but at what cost? In this case, the cost was people leaving your team, with the rest of them gun-shy about working with you, and a long-time vendor threatening to pull out of future events if we don't pay them a premium."

So, what happened here? Marcus was so delighted to finally have Positional Power that he became over-reliant on it. He used the influence tactics of pressure and legitimating, which creates a short-term bump in results based on fear—but has negative impacts on team dynamics.

Former Marine and Goldman Sachs CEO John L. Weinberg has observed, "Tough is easy. Anyone can be tough."[17] When it comes to how to influence others, there's a choice of power and influence tactics to use, and the choice will lead to different results and dynamics. As the saying goes, "If all you have is a hammer, then everything looks like a nail." Too often, we get comfortable with our favorite tactic, and it's easy to choose the comfortable tactic instead of the more effective one. What's needed first is an understanding of what the various influence tactics are, then how they're best used.

Research by Yukl[18] reveals that there are 11 common influence tactics:

1. **Apprising:** Informing the person you're trying to influence of the benefit (for them) of going along with it.

2. **Collaboration:** Working together to obtain a desired result.

3. **Ingratiation:** Doing or saying things to get in the "good graces" of the other person.

4. **Exchange:** Offering something in return for the other person's agreement or help.

5. **Personal Appeals:** Gaining the other person's agreement or help based on who you are and who they are instead of a particular business reason (think of fundraising drives where the CEO makes a "personal appeal").

6. **Coalition Tactics:** Getting others to support your influence attempt.

7. **Consultation:** Requesting expertise or opinion.

8. **Inspirational Appeals:** Arousing strong emotions by linking the influence request to a person's needs, values, hopes, and ideals.

9. **Rational Persuasion:** Making a logical and factual case to support your influence attempt.

10. **Legitimating Tactics:** Reminding the person(s) you're trying to influence that you have the authority to ask and expect compliance with your request by referring to hierarchy, rules, policies, contracts, or precedent. Marcus overused this one.

11. **Pressure:** Use of demands, threats, pestering, or micromanaging—another one of Marcus' favorite tactics.

Out of these 11 influence tactics, four typically create the high levels of commitment associated with engagement: Rational Persuasion, Inspirational Appeals, Collaboration, and Consultation. These are the core influence tactics that serve as the default mode of the Savvy Leader. You can think of it along the lines of the 20/80 rule. These are the 20 percent of influence tactics that Savvy Leaders use 80 percent of the time. Only when circumstances require it, do they use any of the other seven influence tactics, because they would rather put time, energy, and thought into framing their influence in ways that will drive the engagement curve, rather than ways that will induce either the compliance or headwinds curves.

Of the remaining influence tactics, those most likely to create headwinds are Pressure and Legitimating. When faced with someone who uses those tactics, people do just enough to comply without risking their jobs, but you won't see the extra discretionary effort in the mix that comes with the core engagement influence tactics. In some cases, that's acceptable, and a Savvy Leader is aware of the tradeoff instead of being oblivious as to why there is resentful compliance and disengagement.

Are there times when a leader might use the other tactics? You bet, but they should do so with full knowledge of what they may be doing to the team dynamic.

Research by Kipnis et al. reveals that those who take a thoughtful and intentional approach to matching influence tactics to the situation, rather than attempting a one-size-fits-all approach, tend to receive higher work effectiveness scores, enjoy higher salaries, and experience less stress. Why? Because they're using their keen awareness and discretion to adjust to the situation, and that creates fewer headwinds to results and engagement.[19]

Out of the four core influence tactics, Yukl points to one as the most effective overall: Rational Persuasion.[20] Even in this day when we understand the importance of tapping into the emotional side of our teammates, people still want to know "Why?". Think about it; when someone asks you to do something without an obvious reason, isn't there an initial thought or reaction to ask why? When people are given the reason why, it adds purpose to the request. In Chapter 6, we saw that purpose is a primary way to enhance motivational engagement.

This is another time when it's important to be tuned into your organization's culture and the people you're trying to influence. Some cultures and people are much more receptive to being influenced when there's a solid, well-reasoned case made from Rational Persuasion. A Savvy Leader will dial it up for that type of culture. Even when dealing with an organizational culture with less of an emphasis on Rational Persuasion, there may be certain people to whom it is more important. You're much more likely to be effective when influencing without authority if you make your case with strong Rational Persuasion. When influencing at the peer level or with your direct reports, Rational Persuasion is still part of the equation, but you'll increase your chances of being more effective if you use it in conjunction with one or more of the other three (Inspirational Appeals, Collaboration, and/or Consultation).[21]

It's one thing to decide which influence tactic you'll use; it's another to decide how strongly you're going to use it. Often, leaders don't want to spend the time to more fully develop their influence strategy, and it frequently fails because of that. So when the stakes are high, it's imperative that you do the preparation required to weigh the odds in your favor. For example, you may not care very much which types of pens are purchased for your office (or maybe you do), but you probably *do* care who is hired to be a close colleague.

Eli was the director of advertising at a regional newspaper. His background was in business development, not as a reporter. He was invited to the newspaper's annual strategy session to figure out how they were going to navigate the business waters and grow the newspaper the following year. He was quite excited about this meeting, as he had what he thought were some really innovative ideas about taking the newspaper online (this was back in the early 2000s before YouTube was even a word). He had seen a few other newspapers do this, but it wasn't yet the norm.

The CEO kicked off the meeting by announcing what she thought they should pursue as their strategy for the following year. It was more of the same. The only thing novel about it was that they would get greater rewards (a $10,000 bonus) for executing the strategy and growing the paper that year. Although the extra $10k bonus would be nice, Eli knew that it wasn't the best strategy for the paper at this time in history.

Next up, it was Eli's turn to share his proposal for the strategy. He noted that with the rise of the Internet and a strong trend in further online growth, it made more sense to get out ahead of the trend and take the paper online. They could then offer many more options to their advertisers to get their message out. Though they would still need to write stories, it would cost much less to publish online, and they could outsource the printing as they would be printing only once a week for the weekend edition. It was a very different concept than what the CEO had in mind, and she didn't like his idea. In fact, she rejected it, defended her own idea, and called for a break before moving on to the next person.

Clearly, Eli had failed in his influence attempt. But he was not defeated. He was even more convinced that his proposal was the best one for the newspaper, so he spent the weekend sketching out a side-by-side comparison of the two different business models. Then he consolidated it into a one-page overview of how the two different models were likely to play out. In essence, he strengthened his Rational Persuasion to a point where it was irrefutable unless you simply didn't believe his data.

That Monday, he knocked on the CEO's office door to see if she had a few minutes. He started by falling on his sword and disarming the CEO by saying, "I don't think I did a very good job of explaining my proposal in our meeting last week. I've given it a lot of thought since. Do you have a few minutes to look it over with me?" She agreed to look it over with him. The document showed that they could grow their revenue while also reducing their overhead, which meant much stronger margins for the newspaper and fewer hassles from overhead. Amazed, she asked, "Is this true? Is this really how it would play out?" To which Eli replied humbly, "Yes, based on my research, that is the most likely scenario." She replied emphatically, "We should do this!" and adopted his proposal as the one that would guide their strategy for the next year.

After the year of massive change was over, they had newspapers from all across the nation calling them to ask how they did it and what the results were. They were happy to report that, as they had predicted, they rode the wave of increasing online readership and advertising. They had to make many changes and investments to pull it off that initial year, but in the following years, their margins skyrocketed even as other newspapers were going out of business.

Eli could easily have thrown in the proverbial towel after the CEO rejected his idea. But instead, he increased his Rational Persuasion, added in some Inspirational Appeals, and made some adjustments to account for the CEO's personality and ego. His resolve to strengthen his influence paid off in ways that not only got his idea approved but very likely saved his job and those of everyone else at the organization (except the printing department) because they were then on a sustainable path to grow the paper.

Savvy Leaders emphasize Rational Persuasion, and also know when to take it to the next level of due diligence based on the level of risk or opportunity that they're presented with. Savvy Leaders also know when to back off. There are times where you can win the battle but lose the war by compulsively proving yourself, which will turn people off before you even have a chance to begin.

Now that we know what the core four influence tactics are, and know that we can dial them up or down depending on the circumstances, let's take a look at some suggestions for how to use each of them.

Rational Persuasion

Strong Rational Persuasion tends to focus on information. Organizations are increasingly striving to be "data-driven." With the wealth of data being accumulated through technology and made available through the Cloud, it's easier than ever to find data to support what you're trying to prove; often, it's right under your nose. Data can be found in internal measurements as well as benchmarking examples. The latter can be found by searching online, then used as a precedent, making the request less of a novel risk and more of a proven idea (which is especially important for someone low on the OCEAN Openness Scale). In applying the Savvy Rule, using Rational Persuasion would be especially important when working with people who are low on the Agreeableness Scale as well as high on the Conscientiousness Scale.

People who are pitching their company to potential investors make strong use of Rational Persuasion by building business cases to influence their audiences to invest. They also understand that time is limited, so they focus on the most relevant points. Often included in a business case is a SWOT (Strengths, Weaknesses, Opportunities and Threats) analysis to prove they've thought through the market factors.

Another method to help reinforce the strength of Rational Persuasion is the use of graphs. The mere presence of a graph can dramatically increase your persuasive ability. In a research study, two groups of participants were given information about a new pharmaceutical drug. Both were provided with a written explanation of its effectiveness, but with one group, the write-up was accompanied by the simple bar graph.

The result was fascinating: 67.7 percent of the group with no chart believed that the drug was effective. When the researchers added the chart, the percentage of people who believed the drug was effective leaped to 96.6 percent!

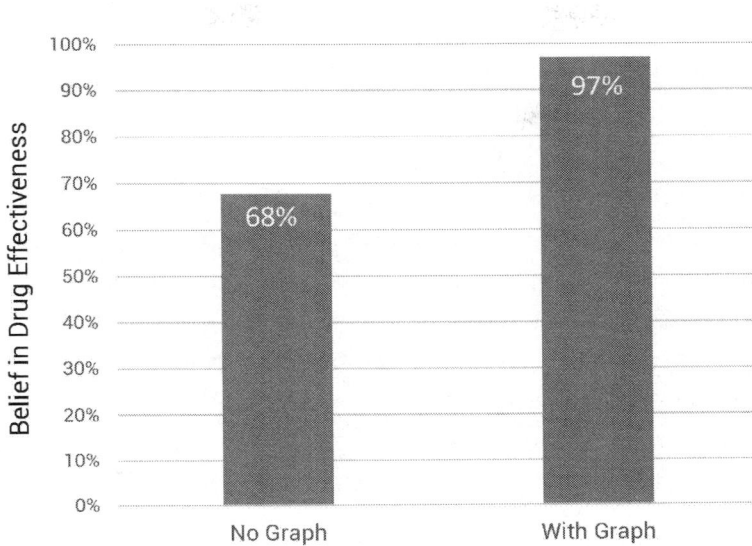

When it comes to the use of graphs for persuasion, seeing really is believing. The authors of the study concluded that when something looks scientific, like a graph, it gains a "scientific halo" that leads people to give it more credence.[22] So when you're developing your Rational Persuasion, consider translating the data visually into a graph to simplify it and give it more credibility. Data visualization company Tableau is growing rapidly because people have realized that being able to understand and interpret data visually makes it more useable and influential. When Eli went to his CEO to re-explain his proposal, he included two graphs to help her visualize the difference.

When you do use data, whether you use graphs or not, make sure you're sharing real, accurate data—because if you start fudging numbers, and people suspect it, you'll lose trust, and your Expert and Personal Power will take a huge hit.

One more way to strengthen your Rational Persuasion is by using the word "because." Researchers studied what happened when someone at an office cut in line to use the copy machine. When the line cutter stated their reason for needing to cut in line as, "Excuse me, I have five pages. May I use the copy machine?" 60 percent of the time people allowed them to cut in line. When they added the word "because" to their reason, asking, "Excuse me, I have five pages. May I use the copy machine *because* I'm in a rush?" the percentage of people who allowed them to cut in line increased to 94 percent.

Interestingly, when they asked it this way, "Excuse me, I have five pages. May I use the copy machine, because I have to make some copies?" (a lame reason, but using the word "because"), the percentage of people who allowed them to cut in line was 93 percent! That's almost as high as when they had a legitimate reason ("I'm in a rush"). Granted, as the request became more substantial (like making a 50-page request), the rates of compliance decreased, but still trended significantly higher when the word "because" was used as part of the request.[23]

Willingness to Allow Line Cutting at Copy Machine

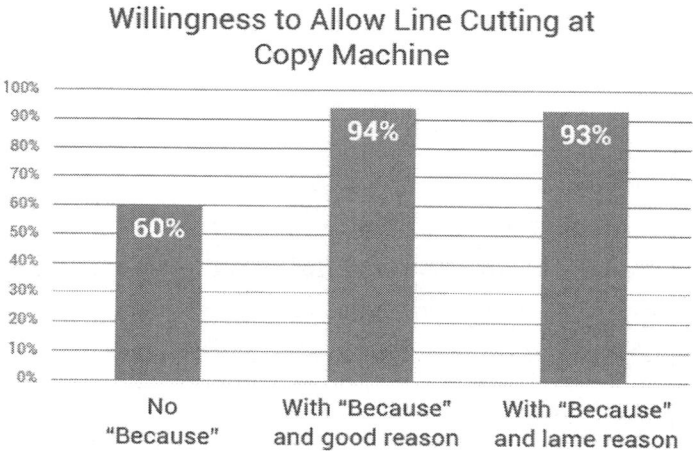

No "Because"	With "Because" and good reason	With "Because" and lame reason
60%	94%	93%

Why does this occur? Because "because" is a trigger for Rational Persuasion. People are inherently more open to influence when there's a rational reason (and less likely to push back, as they may not have developed a credible counter-argument). It goes back to the purpose part of motivational engagement and providing the "why." I've even seen this at play with my kids playing in the kiddie pool in the backyard. My son wanted my daughter to get out of the pool, but when he asked her to move, she resisted. Then he strengthened his request by using better Rational Persuasion, "Can you please move out of the pool because I want to jump into it without running into you?" and she said, "Oh, okay," and stepped out of the pool.

One caveat—using the statement "Because I said so" doesn't count, as it comes off as a legitimating tactic that's likely to create headwinds.

As with any of the core influence tactics, sincerity is important. Have you ever had an experience where someone tried to influence you, but they weren't being intellectually honest? When we realize it, defensiveness is a common reaction. But when people acknowledge the fuller picture, the defensiveness tends to decrease. It's a mechanism similar to empathy: people want their view of reality understood. Even if it's not agreed with, they're more willing to trust those who understand them. Without sincerity and intellectual honesty, you're more likely to create unnecessary headwinds than reduce them. A lack of sincerity and intellectual honesty also degrades the nature of the interaction, so it feels more "gamey" than real, which is why politicians often create headwinds.

Inspirational Appeals

As I mentioned earlier, Inspirational Appeals focus on connecting to people's emotions, values, and ideals. If Rational Persuasion is focused on the head, then Inspirational Appeals are focused on the heart. Leaders often use Inspirational Appeals to get people emotionally excited about a potential change because it means something *more* than just change— it means moving closer to an ideal, or better alignment with a value. Martin Luther King, Jr.'s "I Have a Dream" speech is a great example of using Inspirational Appeals to influence massive social change. While he could have focused on trying to convince people using purely Rational Persuasion, it was much more powerful to focus on Inspirational Appeals. He compelled both the head and the heart.

If you're struggling with trying to figure out how to use Inspirational Appeals, a simple way is by using stories. Inspirational stories include the problem and its impacts. Then move to the resolution and what that would be like, ending with a call to action. A great example of this is former Vice President and presidential candidate turned climate change activist Al Gore. During the presidential debates, he was widely criticized for being robotic and stiff. To his credit, he took that feedback to heart. While it was too little too late for his presidential campaign, he emerged years later as a charismatic speaker. His passion was educating people about climate change. He received coaching from Nancy Duarte, an expert on how to tell a compelling story. He created the documentary/ slide show "An Inconvenient Truth," and came to life with stories that tapped into the influence tactic of Inspirational Appeals. Democrats and Republicans alike were amazed at the transformation in his ability to influence people.

How might you unintentionally create headwinds when using Inspirational Appeals? By not resonating with your audience, because you're either unaware of what inspires them, or you are aware and simply didn't make the appropriate adjustments. For example, the rivalry between the New York Yankees and the Boston Red Sox is considered one of the greatest in American sports. There's no love lost between these two teams and their fan bases. They even have historical events and curses as part of their legendary rivalry (like the Red Sox trading Babe Ruth to the New York Yankees and the Yankees going on to win 27 World Series, while it took until 2004 for the famous "Curse of the Bambino" to be broken when the Red Sox finally won their first World Series).

Now, what if you grew up in New York and you were a Yankees fan? Let's say that as part of your work, you had to travel to Boston to give a presentation about the project you were working on, but during that meeting you used a positive example involving the Yankees. That wouldn't be inspiring for the average Red Sox fan. I've seen this happen with other sports teams. A certain percentage of people will laugh it off, but another group will get defensive and mad rather than inspired. It may have been funny for the people who laughed, but you probably lost the others. So be sure that what inspires you is also inspiring to your audience. Otherwise, you'll create unnecessary headwinds.

Consultation

Consultation is the requesting of expertise or opinion. When done well, it can be a very effective influence tactic. There are several things that Savvy Leaders do when they use Consultation to influence others. First, they're clear on what they're using their influencing for, and they make sure that it's aligned with what they're consulting about ("Can you help me think this situation through?", "How do you think this proposal would be received by your leader?", etc.). Savvy Leaders actively listen instead of treating Consultation as just a means to an end. They give empathy and are engaged in the moment because they understand that they're probably receiving some really helpful nuggets of information.

When receiving advice, people often feel the pressure to either accept it all or reject it all. There's a motto that Savvy Leaders use that helps them sift through the information: "Eat the meat and spit out the bones." Be open and eager to find what's valuable, and disregard what's not. If someone senses your willingness to wrestle with what they're saying rather than rejecting it outright by saying things like, "That would never work," or "We've tried that before," then they'll be more willing to consult with you again in the future. Plus, they'll be more engaged.

Requesting Consultation can even influence your odds of being recommended for a promotion! Research reveals that if an employee is receiving an underwhelming or even hostile performance evaluation, if instead of getting defensive they ask for advice, the likelihood of them being recommended for promotion jumps from 31 percent to 58 percent.

Why does this occur? Because when you ask for advice out of sincere curiosity and a desire to learn and grow, your response is met first of all with relief because you

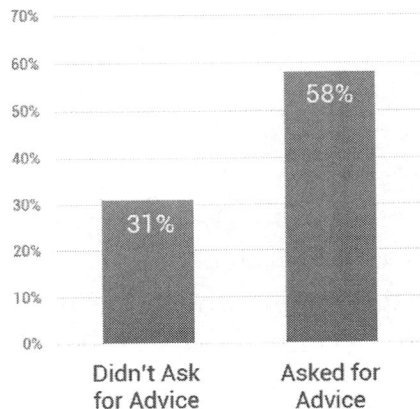

70%	
60%	
50%	58%
40%	
30%	
20%	31%
10%	
0%	
Didn't Ask for Advice	Asked for Advice

didn't become defensive. It also triggers empathy towards you, and the critic is more willing to invest in you because of your cooperation and eagerness to develop. Additionally, it makes them feel honored that you're asking them for their advice.[24]

Jonah was a new leader of a product development team. His team had a new concept that they thought could be really successful. While he believed in the strength of the concept, he needed the resources of the company to bring it to life. The company had many similar projects going on, and internal competition for resources was high. He realized that Sarah, who was the leader of a technical team, would be a very important person approve this project, as it would take a lot of effort from her team to pull it off. He analyzed the situation through the stakeholder quadrant and realized that Sarah was likely in the "Latent" category: able to make things happen, but not currently interested in the project (in fact, it wasn't even on her radar).

Knowing Sarah was at the peer level, Jonah decided to use the influence tactic of Consultation to get her on board. He invited her to a meeting and used thoughtfully prepared Rational Persuasion and Inspirational Appeals to describe the importance of the project to the customers. He explained that he needed two things from her to make it happen—one being her Consultation, the other being her approval. She agreed to do the initial Consultation right then and there. After they talked it through, she decided to green light the project for her team, and to prioritize it.

Jonah's straightforward use of Consultation helped Sarah see the value of the project and put her personal stamp on it, creating a sense of ownership. She was delighted to be involved, and they successfully brought the product to market just four months later.

Given the great benefits possible from using Consultation, let's look at a how some have used it in a way that created unnecessary headwinds instead. The most common way that people create headwinds is by using Consultation in a disingenuous way. If your sole reason for using Consultation is to influence someone to help you, while not truly being open to being influenced yourself, the other person will most likely sense it and feel like they're being played. When that happens, you lose trust, engagement, and opportunity. Savvy Leaders use Consultation not only to get buy-in and influence but also so that they can truly learn.

Collaboration

Collaboration is the invitation to "co-labor" in order to bring an idea to fruition or to get work done. As with consultation, Savvy Leaders align their Collaboration requests with what they're trying to influence. People who are good at Collaboration are clear about what they want to collaborate on, and how the decisions and work will be divided up. Savvy Leaders use Collaboration to influence people in ways like offering to help them with any problems that arise out of their agreement to collaborate, offering to bring in extra resources to get the job done, and even teaching their co-workers how to do their parts of the job. Any of these can help people be more open to influence through Collaboration.

As you use Collaboration to influence others, it's important to first understand how people view Collaboration in your organizational culture. Some organizations have a ruthless, every-man-for-himself tone, whereas others—especially many of the younger companies—have a strong sense of Collaboration intentionally built into their culture. Understanding where your organization is on that spectrum informs how you approach people to collaborate. If you find yourself in a culture that's already collaborative, using Collaboration to influence should be fairly simple. If you find yourself in one of the Lone Ranger, old-school cultures, you'll need to make some adjustments. For example, don't be soft in your request to collaborate; be assertive, keep it focused on business results, and help the other person understand how collaborating will benefit them as well. Of course, knowing where they are on the OCEAN Personality Scale can help you dial it in even further, especially knowing their degree of agreeableness (or lack thereof).

Research has revealed an interesting way to create a stronger collaborative dynamic. It's a word that readies the mind for collaboration and grit: "together." An experiment was conducted where people in one group were told they were working "together" with people in another room and would receive tips from them, even though the tips were actually manufactured by the researchers. In the other group, individuals were told they were working alone, but would receive tips from the researchers. Astoundingly, those who were told that they were working "together" with other people in another room:

- Persisted in working 48 percent longer.

- Solved more problems.

- Had better recall.

- Felt less tired.

Why is the word "together" so powerful? It seems that it creates an innate sense of accountability, along with a greater desire to help the team and not to be the weak link and disappoint others.[25]

Keep in mind that one of the best ways to collaborate and influence people is to decide who will decide. When a decision needs to be made, most of the time the best person to make that decision isn't the boss; it's the employee closest to the issue.

That's why Savvy Leaders are often decisive in an unusual way—they decide they aren't the right person to make a decision... and then decide who is. They do it not because they don't want to avoid making certain decisions, but because they know they *shouldn't* make certain decisions. For example, instead of deciding whether to expedite shipping, a Savvy Leader may decide who's in the best position to make that decision, and put her in charge. Deciding who will decide fosters greater engagement, greater empowerment, helps employees not just take responsibility but take ownership... and is an excellent example of how Savvy Leaders use indirect influence as well as direct influence.

Naturally, there are ways to derail the effectiveness of Collaboration and turn it into a headwind. One of the most common is by making a disingenuous request for Collaboration. A common example is a leader talking to a direct report and saying, "We need to fix this," which the direct report (if they're perceptive and reading between the lines) knows really means: *I don't want to ask you directly, but please make sure that YOU fix this.* When leaders use Collaboration this way, it creates unnecessary headwinds by being incongruent with what they truly mean, which diminishes relational engagement and trust. It can even become an office joke, where people outside the earshot of the leader say to each other sarcastically, "WEEEEE need to fix this!"

Collaboration works well to influence when used with good, clean intent.

Summary

While power and influence are key to making things happen, they can also easily create a stifling effect that results in unnecessary headwinds. It's the job of the leader, not their direct reports, to be aware of this and to increase their leadership savvy so they reduce the unnecessary headwinds based on how they exercise their power and influence. Not only does that reduce the potential downside of the J-Curve, it also provides the foundation for a higher upside to enhance engagement and ultimately drive results.

Action Steps

- Determine your default influence tactic. Then be honest: how well does your default influence tactic work for you? Do you get the results you expect? Are your employees not just high-performing but also highly engaged?

- Now determine which core four influence tactic would better meet the needs of your team (make sure you refer to the answers to the Savvy Rules questions.) Forget how you *like* to influence people: what influence tactic would be most effective?

- List specific situations where you can use a different influence tactic and commit to using that approach. Evaluate the results, adjust where necessary... and rinse and repeat.

SECTION
FOUR

OPTIMIZING
FOR RESULTS

- Preparation

- Assertiveness

- Challenging Conversations

CHAPTER 9

Preparation and Assertiveness

> "Only those who will risk going too far
> can possibly find out how far one can go."
>
> —T. S. Eliot,
> British poet

At the end of the day, you'll be judged by your team by how you lead, and judged by your leader by what you produce. It's a tension that many people feel is an either/or proposition, but fortunately, what works well for people also tends to produce better results. What we've covered in this book already provides you with a leadership playbook to create a dynamic for high-performance results, and yet, there are a few more important factors that can help push your results over the tipping point of success.

Preparation

Daniel is a fantastic public speaker. He's not a rah-rah motivational speaker, but he connects with his audience in a very personal way. He always gets rave reviews wherever he goes. I once talked with him at dinner after he'd delivered another dynamic session, and asked him how he does it. He said, "What you didn't see was the twenty-five hours of prep I did this week, or the two hours of rehearsal I did last night, or the numerous coaching sessions I've had in my career to improve my ability to do what you saw me do in forty-five minutes today." You don't always have the luxury of time to prepare thoroughly for everything, but in many cases you do. I've witnessed far too many sales calls where people tried to wing it by just jumping on the phone or into a meeting without doing any due diligence beforehand. Most times, the client can tell, and it erodes Expert Power fast. There are times when we have to get important things done, and it's essential that we prepare for those to an extra degree. There's a saying that luck is where opportunity and preparation meet. If you're prepared, you'll be able to take advantage of opportunities that less-prepared people will miss out on.

Assertiveness

The second way of optimizing results is by adjusting your level of assertiveness.

Lee was a leader at a large technology company. He was very aggressive, known for pushing his team so hard that results often came at the cost of sustainable workloads. After he had his first few successes, he felt his style was effective, even if he wouldn't get the Boss of the Year award anytime soon. He even got a promotion within his first year, based on the output of his team. What the company wasn't measuring was the engagement level of the team. In his second year, his aggressive leadership style began to have diminishing returns. People had had enough of working for him. He was smart and knew how to push, but he was pushing people too hard, and they were disengaging. They would do just enough to keep their jobs, while looking for an internal transfer or even a move to another company. By the middle of his second year, turnover on his team had reached 45 percent, versus the company average of 18 percent.

His leader noticed this and realized he had a problem on his hands that was about to significantly reduce Lee's ability to perform. Clearly, what got him results in his first year wasn't going to work in his second year at the company. So his leader shared the information with him, but also shared some helpful research about levels of assertiveness and how it effects a leader's results.

Researchers examined a leader's level of assertiveness and how frequently they used that level of assertiveness. [26] They then compared the results to leaders who had failed and ones who were highly effective. They labeled them "Worst Leaders" and "Best Leaders" accordingly. As you can see in the graph below, the worst leaders had a more "U" shaped curve with higher frequency assertiveness at the passive and aggressive ends of the spectrum. The "Best Leaders," on the other hand, had more of an inverted "U" shaped curve with higher frequency of assertiveness in the middle of the spectrum.

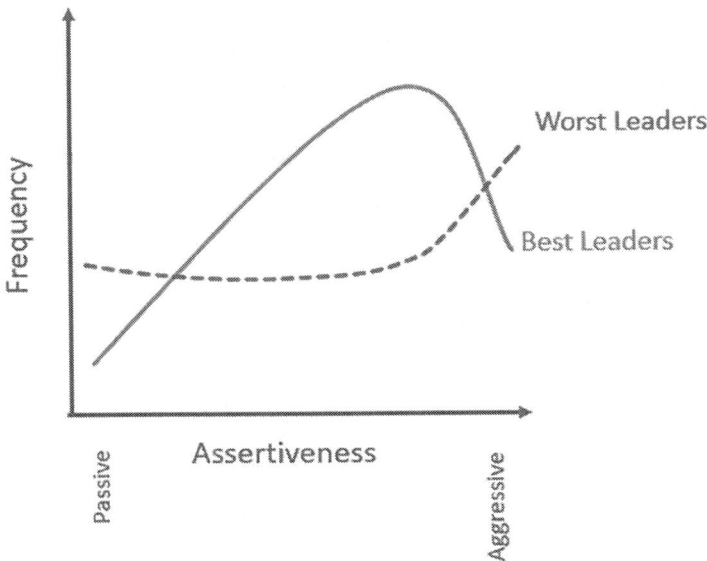

You can imagine an invisible vertical line separating strong assertiveness from aggressiveness, that line being respect. Once that line is crossed, assertiveness suddenly feels like aggression.

The aggressive leader is overly reliant on Legitimate and Coercive Power, which we know typically drives a headwinds dynamic. It can also feel like micromanaging, which does nothing at all for motivational engagement.

On the passive side, it's almost as if the leader has no power or is afraid to use it. People need a leader who sets the direction and doesn't shy away from challenging others to do their best. While we're talking about the leadership dynamic here, that's different than having aggressive goals. Having aggressive goals is great when it matches the potential of the team.

Naturally passive leaders may be tempted to use the excuse "I'm just exhibiting servant leadership," but that's a misapplication of the concept. A servant leader is not a doormat; instead, a servant leader uses their influence as a leader to facilitate growth in others. It's very difficult to do that unless you're willing to dial up your level of assertiveness to thoughtfully speak up and challenge others out of complacency and status quo attitudes. Those are the types of conversations that, while they may be uncomfortable, make an impact and create change.

With the "Best Leaders", it's as if they know that an effective leader drives up to a point, and are cognizant that if they drive beyond that point, they may get a diminishing return and risk creating the headwinds dynamic. "Best Leaders" highest frequency assertiveness level is at the front end of the middle. That is the sweet spot that I call that "Pro-Active Assertiveness." That is where Savvy Leaders camp out. It's the level that they set their assertiveness default to. They also monitor and adjust so that if the situation warrants it, they shift to being more passive or aggressive, but they're strategic about it and recognize the potential consequences of it both on outcomes and dynamics.

In a survey that supports these results, Zenger and Folkman studied whether employees responded better to leaders who were "nice" or leaders who were "tough." Their study looked at 160,576 people working for 30,661 leaders at hundreds of companies, and the results were fascinating. Tough edged out nice by 8.9 percent to 6.7 percent in terms of producing high engagement.

However, the real surprise was when they asked not if workers preferred a leader who was nice *or* tough, but if they preferred someone who was nice *and* tough. Then the engagement numbers swelled to 68 percent![27]

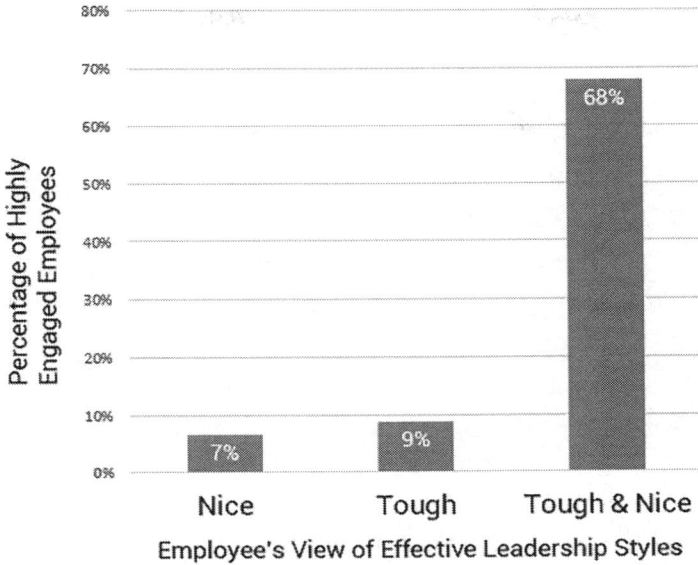

Employee's View of Effective Leadership Styles

The researchers conclude that leaders trying to drive productivity shouldn't be afraid to be "nice guys." They do have to demand a lot from their people, but can do so as "great developers of people" in ways that are "consistent, trusting, and collaborative." Clearly, the Savvy Leader wins by motivating their people and driving for results. Again, assertiveness is important, especially when it's balanced by sincere attempts to engage and motivate the worker via positive uses of power and influence.

A Savvy Leader understands that they need to adjust the throttle of assertiveness depending on the team they're working with. If the team is highly motivated and on the right track, the leader can dial their assertiveness back and take a more hands-off/empowering posture. If the team is doing unethical things—like the team of engineers at Volkswagen who installed the "defeat device" that tricked the EPA into thinking that their diesel engines were clean, when in fact they were spewing pollution—that would be a situation where the leader should push beyond assertiveness in order to send a message and quickly shut down that type of behavior. The default mode of Savvy Leaders is at the more proactive side of assertiveness, where you challenge people to perform and they feel motivated by it, instead of going over the tipping point where they feel resentful and start disengaging. Is it a balancing act? You bet! But at least you know what to aim for.

In Lee's case, though he was embarrassed and frustrated with himself, he was also coachable. He took the information to heart and moderated his level of assertiveness. He still held the bar high for results, but made a commitment to lead with respect. That alone helped set a new tone for his team; the poor numbers started to reverse, and productivity went up.

Lee's situation is a common one, because most leaders aren't taught how assertive they should be, and how assertiveness connects to motivation, engagement and performance. Often leaders feel the pressure for results, fear of failure kicks in, and they easily cross the respect line from proactively assertive to aggressive. Being aggressive can feel powerful, but it usually has negative long-term consequences for the dynamic and performance of the team. Senior leaders are just as susceptible to this as new leaders are. The challenge for new leaders is to not swing the pendulum around so wildly. On one hand, there can be a hesitancy to step into the power position of being the new leader and being assertive; on the other, new leaders sometimes take it too far, marginalizing their team by exercising too much Legitimate Power for too long.

Whereas seasoned leaders may "land softly" to build rapport and strengthen their awareness before they become more assertive, many first-time leaders push the lever the other way, so people will respect their new authority; but then they throttle it back, so they can drive the engagement curve dynamic. Either way, it's a variable that defaults to proactively assertive with adjustments for specific situations.

Women and Assertiveness

Using assertiveness effectively takes some diligence and savvy. This is particularly true for women where there is frequently an unwelcome double standard, but ignoring it won't help. Take Emily, for example.

She was a regional sales director for a large hotel company. It was a very numbers-driven sales organization, where you were only as good as yesterdays' results. In order to maintain her role and have the opportunity to advance, she needed to grow her sales numbers. She had enough experience to understand that people often react poorly to assertive women in the workplace, and that it can create a headwinds dynamic. Knowing the power of assertiveness to drive or derail performance, she was savvy about how she used it. For starters, she monitored and adjusted her level of assertiveness, depending on the situation and the people involved, knowing that a one-size-fits-all approach wouldn't be nearly as effective. Understanding that she needed feedback to know how she was coming across, she sought out a discerning and honest member of the team to help her dial it in.

Her team came up against the common problems that face all sales teams—increasing quotas, long sales cycles, recruiting and training, not-so-subtle jabs from executives about sales affecting stock prices, etc. She navigated her team through all those challenges by being a Savvy Leader, especially in terms of her leadership assertiveness. Within six months, her team had increased their sales more than any other team in the country. She was placed in the succession plan for her leader because of the results she was able to achieve, and how she achieved them.

This example illustrates a common predicament and opportunity for women who use assertiveness in the workplace. For men it's much simpler; in general, they're allowed more latitude in how hard they drive for results, whereas women are often in a double-bind. If they drive too hard, they face a backlash effect and get labeled a jerk—or worse. If they don't push enough, they can't drive results. So how do you navigate this minefield?

First and foremost, be savvy about how you use assertiveness to drive results. Research by O'Neil & O'Reilly has unlocked a secret of effective assertiveness for women in the workplace. The key difference is their self-awareness and their adjustment of their assertiveness levels to match each situation. In other words, savvy female leaders know when to dial it up or down. The research found that women who were highly assertive and self-aware enough to make adjustments to their style received one-and-a-half times as many promotions as highly assertive men, regardless of the men's level of self-awareness. Interestingly, they were also three times more likely to receive a promotion than women who were highly assertive but not very self-aware.[28]

It's one thing to know the connection between self-awareness, assertiveness, and effectiveness; it's another to develop it. In the example above, Emily realized this dilemma, so she made a savvy move by finding a colleague who would give her feedback on her assertiveness, which would then enable her to make proper adjustments. Because we're often not very good at knowing how we're perceived, it's extremely valuable to increase self-awareness with feedback. I've also seen leaders ask their teams in one-on-one conversations how they perceive them—not in an insecure way, but in a curious, open way with a sincere intent to use the feedback to improve. I've seen others who were so mindful of the difference this dynamic could make to their leadership effectiveness and promotability that they self-initiated a full 360 review, so they could get an entirely anonymous perspective from their leader, colleagues and direct reports alike.

The other thing that Emily worked on was her presence. She proactively adjusted her posture, lowered the pitch of voice when there was a tendency to anxiously raise it, didn't make statements seem as if they were questions from an insecure person, was direct in her language, managed her emotions, and was confident as she led. She also maintained an amazing warmth and enjoyment for her people and the work that they did, which put them at ease with her leadership. It wasn't easy to manage these variables in addition to the others that we cover in this book, but the more she did it, the more natural it became, and in her case it literally paid off.

And not only did it pay off personally for Emily, but her growth as a leader also benefitted her team as well. Savvy Leaders model how to adjust the throttle of assertiveness, setting an example for their direct reports who are or aspire to be in leadership positions. Ultimately, how most people lead is, at least in part, a reflection of how they have been led. That's why it's not just important for *you* to become a Savvy Leader but for you to show, by example, how other people can, too. Not only do those individuals benefit, but the entire organization benefits as well. In time, you can help create a culture base filled with Savvy Leaders driving operational results while better meeting the extrinsic and intrinsic needs of every employee.

Win-win!

Action Steps

- Consider your preparedness habits. Can you think of a specific circumstance where you nailed it? (Of course you can.)

- Can you think of a specific circumstance where you failed? (That may not seem as easy—but everyone has.)

- Write down what you did or did not do that caused you to fail. Then determine what you should have done differently, and commit to always doing what's necessary to nail it.

- Then determine the ways you monitor your assertiveness (or whether you even try.) Commit to critiquing yourself on a regular basis, or better yet, asking a trusted colleague to give you regular feedback—and to providing that same kind of feedback to your colleague.

CHAPTER 10

Challenging Conversations

> "You've got to go out on a limb sometimes,
> because that's where the fruit is."
>
> —WILL ROGERS,
> AMERICAN HUMORIST

When organizations are surveyed about their development needs, the number one need is usually better communication. How communication happens has a strong connection to how committed and engaged people will be as a result. This connection between our perennially low engagement rates and lack of communication is no coincidence; businesses seem adept at doing the same thing repeatedly and expecting different results. So how do we improve our communication in an attempt to drive the engagement J-Curve?

To think about it more specifically, other than email, verbal conversations represent the primary leadership tool of most leaders. They can be big conversations, like a kickoff speech, or smaller but important conversations about expectations or feedback. Ultimately, if you don't improve how you have conversations, the results and dynamics you put into play through conversations won't change for the better. The good news is that improving conversations is fairly simple; it just requires knowing basic conversational structure, and how to pivot it for various uses. Once you learn the base model, you'll learn how to pivot the model to use it for common leadership situations where conversations can make a big difference.

A brief note: I was fortunate to have worked at one of the pioneering conversations training companies early in my career. I logged over 20,000 hours in the field of leadership conversations and came into a deep understanding of the impact that conversations can have on performance and engagement. Many other training companies recognize that impact as well and have joined the conversation chorus with their own unique perspectives and models. Search the term "leadership conversations" online and you'll get over 115 million web results and over 2,500 book results. It's easy to be overwhelmed by all of the choices; what you'll find in this chapter is a model designed to be simple enough to use frequently, agile enough to be used for a variety of different purposes, and robust enough to handle challenging conversations. The two main types of challenging conversations that leaders struggle with are **feedback** and **confrontation**.

Let's learn the model first, and then we'll look at how it pivots. We call this the **5 i Conversation Model**. The sequencing of this model is psychologically important because it helps create a dynamic where people are more likely to engage in the conversation and make it more productive. So let's look at each of the five "I's" in sequence.

Intent

Intent is important in three ways. First, you need to be grounded in your intent. As you examine your true intent, it's important to know if the reason for having the conversation is for ego—that is, reasons of proving your expertise or power—or if it's genuinely intended to help the other person. If you find that your intent is self-serving, stop. If you have the conversation with the other person from an ego-based intent, they'll quickly pick up on it, and you'll find the conversation driving the headwinds dynamic.

The second way that intent factors into conversations is in examining what you believe the other person's intent to be. Leaders often mistakenly begin with the assumption that a person they need to speak with has malicious intent. If that's the assumption the leader makes, it sets up a negative mental roadmap in their mind, and the chances of it leading to successful change are diminished because of that low ceiling. Leaders tend to find a healthier dynamic when they assume either benign or positive intent on the part of the other person. The vast majority of people aren't "out to get" others; they simply may not realize how their behavior is impacting other people, or they may have a different style, culture, or personality that leads to the friction.

That said, a Savvy Leader is also aware that in a small percentage of situations, the person may, in fact, have bad intent, either because of a personal or psychological issue or simply because they feel they were wronged in some way and are responding in a vengeful manner. Johann Wolfgang von Goethe struck a wise balance on this issue when he noted,

---

"...misunderstandings and neglect create more confusion in this world than trickery and malice. At any rate, the last two are certainly much less frequent."

Assuming good intent can add resilience to the conversation because it can help you weather a defensive reaction. It's also important to realize that your body language will communicate to the other person(s) your assumption of their intent. If you have an open body posture and are leaning slightly forward with sincere interest, it will send a very different signal than if you have your arms folded, are leaning back, and have a look of suspicion in your eyes.

The third way in which intent plays a role is that it announces to the other person what type of conversation you intend to have, instead of leaving them to their own assumptions. Often people go to a dark place in their minds, assuming they're about to be fired or disciplined. One of the most important elements in a conversation is a sense of safety. When the intent of the conversation is unknown or unclear, people tend to stay in a heightened state of anxiety. Knowing the intent helps the receiver categorize the conversation and view it through the appropriate lens, instead of trying to figure out what kind of conversation it is. By announcing intent at the start of the conversation, you enable them to enter into the conversation more quickly. I'll show you specifics of how to do this as we get into some examples later in the chapter.

Issue

The second "I" is *issue*. After laying a foundation for the type of conversation by sharing your intent, the next step is to share the issue you want to talk about. This is an important step, one that you don't want to do on the fly. Spend some time preparing beforehand, so you're realistic, specific, and succinct in explaining the issue. Using examples helps the other person wrap their heads around what you're talking about. In describing the issue, whenever possible make use of "I" rather than "you" statements, to reduce defensiveness, because the unbalanced use of "you" can feel like someone is verbally pointing a finger in your face. At some point, you'll need to say "you" in the issue statement; just don't say it more than you need to.

Other words to be wary of are "always" and "never." Most times, the black-and-white nature of always/never doesn't hold up to scrutiny. There's often an exception where someone did or didn't do something that breaks the absolute certainty of these words. Because of that, their use is perceived as intellectually dishonest and shuts down authentic conversation.

If you truly want to have a conversation that makes a difference, it has to be honest and sincere—and people can usually tell when it isn't. Another nuanced way to start the issue statement is to use the term "I've noticed..." rather than a more abrupt variant like "Whenever...."

Importance

The third "I" is *importance*. When people know why the issue is important, it helps make their participation in the conversation more relevant, and their desire for resolution more compelling. If the issue doesn't have a significant level of importance, or they remain unaware of its importance, then you aren't likely to acquire their full attention and energy towards resolving the issue. If you can help them understand the connection between their behavior and business impacts, it will make the importance of the conversation more relevant to their work and less about a personal conflict.

Inquire

The fourth "I" is *inquire*. Now that the receiver has a solid understanding of your intent, what the issue is, and why it's important, your job is to get curious and ask them for their thoughts. Inquiry is both a mindset and an action. The mindset part is about being open and sincerely curious. When you truly come from a place of genuine, open curiosity, it lends the conversation to a more collaborative dynamic, which ultimately leads to more sustainable results and a better dynamic during and after the conversation.

During this phase in the model, it's also important to keep the conversation from closing too fast. There may be a temptation to close quickly, because of our emphasis on the value of efficiency and because of some of the natural discomfort that may accompany such conversations. But you're the leader in this. You set the tone with your intent; you laid out the issue and why it's important; now you have to lead by being the resilient explorer in this conversation and by asking questions.

Imagine what the world would be like if no one ever explored. What if they took a day hike on a new island and said, "That's it, I've seen enough, let's move on?" They might miss an amazing treasure buried in a cave. The same is true of conversations; successful salespeople are masters of exploratory conversation. The goal is not to draw out the conversation unnecessarily, but instead to make it long enough so that the other person has time to recover from their initial fight-or-flight reaction. Then they can settle into a de-escalated mode, where they're better able to explore, reflect, and be vulnerable. If they sense a lack of psychological safety, they will resist and hide their truth. It's part of your job in leading the conversation to provide that space through your mindset, words, and non-verbal cues, knowing they may still be on edge, but you've done your part to provide an environment where a productive conversation can occur.

Some argue that it's the other person's job to speak up in tough situations, regardless of the degree of psychological safety; others argue that it's the leader's role to make it safe enough for the team member to speak up. I agree with both arguments—it's a bit of a chicken-or-egg scenario—but the greater onus is on the leader to set a dynamic where others feel safe enough, and then proactively draw them out. Sincere questions are a powerful tool for doing that. When people do speak up, it's important to honor the courage they're exemplifying by hearing them out without shooting the messenger, no matter how strong a knee-jerk reaction you have to the message. If people aren't speaking up to you as a leader, it's important to understand why.

I'll help you dismiss one reason: it's not because everything is "fine." Dig deeper, with sincere curiosity.

Implement

The fifth "I" is *implement*. Now that you've had a substantial conversation, it's time to ensure that it translates it into action. Have you ever been to a training session that was good, but you never really did much with what you learned because there was no implementation plan? The same is true with significant conversations. Without the implementation and follow-through, a good conversation will remain just a good conversation, with little to show for it except for lots of wasted energy.

While it's often best to do this collaboratively, there are also circumstances where, as the leader, you take the lead in creating the implementation plan, while the other person(s) in the conversation commits to it. The components of the implementation plan will vary depending on the circumstance, but in general, you want to make sure that it is clear, makes a difference, and includes a mechanism for follow-through. You can use a simple tool that project leaders frequently use to create accountable action. It's represented by the acronym WWW, which stands for "**WHO does WHAT WHEN?**" If there are multiple items on the action list, you can even create a WWW chart to record it. Of course, as the leader, you'll want to be proactive in circling back to ensure that they completed their action plan.

Here are the 5 i's in the order in which you should use them:

1. **intent**

2. **issue**

3. **importance**

4. **inquiry**

5. **implementation**

Now that you have an understanding of the base model, let's look at how to pivot the model to use it for coaching feedback and confrontation. One of the main variables that contributes to the pivot is the degree of assertiveness used.

Feedback

Feedback in the workplace is an important tool for developing workers. It's become even more important with the Millennial generation in the workforce; they tend to be more used to feedback, and many of them crave it. Think about social media: it's built around sharing and feedback. It has wired the younger generations to expect a steady stream of feedback through comments and "likes" (or lack thereof). When there is no feedback, it feels like throwing a rock in a cave where there's no echo. Without proactive, consistent feedback, it's easy for things to head in the wrong direction, where results are diminished, and a more significant confrontation has to occur. Regularly providing feedback reduces the chances of things escalating to the point where you need to confront. While we often think of feedback in a negative way, it's also important to provide positive feedback.

Remember earlier in the book, when we talked about the Magic Ratio? For people to maintain a healthy relationship in the workplace, a good rule of thumb is that for every negative interaction, there must be three positive ones to fill the tank. That doesn't mean they'll all happen in the same conversation, as that can confuse the issue, but overall it's an important factor to keep in mind.

When providing feedback, you need enough assertiveness to make the conversation happen, but not so much that the person you're giving feedback to feels like you're bowling them over with it. With the feedback, you also want to open up the conversation, so there's space for them have their own realizations about the issue. We all have blind spots, and when someone provides feedback, it helps fill in the blank so we can do something about it. A feedback conversation might look something like this:

1. **intent:** *I'd like to provide you with some feedback that I think will help you in your career here. Do you have some time to talk?*

2. **issue:** *I've noticed that when the senior leaders visit the office, you seem more reserved around them. For example, last time they were here you simply said "Hello" to them and declined their invitation to join them for lunch.*

3. **importance:** *The reason why I bring this up is because I know you're a strong team member, and you'd like to get promoted soon, but they question your promotability because of what they perceive as a lack of social skills.*

4. **inquiry:** *So what's going on behind the scenes with you when they visit?*

5. **implementation:** *Given all that, what are you going to commit to doing to ensure that the next time they show up, you'll act in a more social way?* (You can use the WWW method here to clarify accountable action).

You'll notice that there's a certain amount of proactive assertiveness included in this discussion on the part of the leader. But it's not forcing the issue; it's offering it up. It's from someone who cares about the other person and wants to help them, but also wants them to own what they do with it. They're willing to bring it up and facilitate the conversation, but they aren't going to force the other person to do anything with it. This type of conversation is the kind that can help people feel the push for continual improvement that creates more motivated workers, as long as it's not being used in a micromanaging or hyper-critical way, as people also have a balancing drive for empowerment.

Confrontation

Karl has never been the most detail-oriented person, but this time it cost his team and the company a significant opportunity. Karl is a sales engineer. He partners with the sales team to create live demos of their technology so that potential clients can see the custom solution for their payroll system. Karl has been in his role for six years now and is confident that he can pull off just about anything. His confidence has grown to the point where he doesn't put in extra time like he used to; instead, he wings it.

Karl flew with his sales colleague, Simone, to Chicago to meet with her client, a medium-sized packaging company. They got into the conference room a bit early and got all their technology set up. The client joined them, and after Simone shared with them what they were able to do, she turned it over to Karl, and he opened up the application on the big flat screen at the end of the room. He got an error message, which he secretly thought was weird, so he restarted the system and got the same error message again. This time, he blamed the client, saying, "Oh, there must be an issue with your corporate firewall," which was just grasping at straws. So he shut down his computer and said he would be glad to do a live demo remotely when he got back to the office the following day. The client was polite but underwhelmed, and you could see it in their posture as they said goodbye.

Back in the office the next day, Karl couldn't figure out what had happened. He called the technology vendor, and they said that they had sent him and all of their other clients an urgent action email the previous week, giving them a warning that there was a malware bug in their system and instructing everyone to update their application. He said he didn't receive it. Then he went into his email "spam" box, and sure enough, there it was. He was quite embarrassed and fessed up to Simone. Simone wasn't pleased and mentioned it to Karl's leader, Elana.

Elana had noted Karl's tendency to become more cavalier about the details over the years (FYI, he was also low on the OCEAN Conscientiousness scale) and though it concerned her, she'd written off doing anything about it before because, in spite of it, he was a solid sales engineer. But this was a big deal, and she had to confront him to ensure that it didn't happen again.

She used the 5 i Conversation Model and made the pivot for using it for confrontation. Here's how it looked:

1. **intent:** *Karl, I want to have a conversation with you about something that needs to change.*

2. **issue:** *I've noticed your tendency to not prepare as much as you need to for client demos. For example, what happened yesterday with the client in Chicago was a very preventable problem if you had been better prepared.*

3. **importance:** *It's important to prepare, because when you don't, it comes off as disrespectful to the teammates who work hard to land every demo. And unfortunately, in this situation, I just found out from the client that they are no longer interested in our solution.*

4. **inquire:** *So let's talk. Why is this happening? What's going on behind the scenes for you?* (Be sincerely curious, as it might uncover some hidden issues.)

5. **implementation:** *Let's talk about how you can ensure that from here on out each demo has meticulous preparation so that it goes flawlessly.* (Before the conversation is over, use the WWW "Who does What When" method to ensure that there's a specific action plan in place for the changed behavior).

At first, Karl was defensive, but he was relieved that this wasn't a firing conversation; instead, it was one that was intended to solve the problem that he had created. When Karl sensed that Elana didn't just want the right answer, she sincerely wanted the *real* answer, and that it was okay to share it, he opened up. He apologized for what had happened and felt bad for everyone involved. He confessed that he was growing bored in his current role, and felt he needed some variety. Elana shared with him the concept of flow that we covered in Chapter 6, and they talked about options for new challenges which both excited him and would be a step out of his comfort zone. Elana also brought the conversation back to his current role and asked him what he could do in the meantime to ensure that this type of a scenario didn't repeat itself.

Karl had some great ideas, and Elana pressed him to decide on a few that would best resolve the issue and that he could commit to doing. He decided on a few, and Elana asked him the scaling question—which, by the way, is a great tool to get people to take an extra step towards a solution. She asked him, "These sound like good steps. On a scale of one to ten, how confident are you that they will resolve the issue?"

Karl replied, "Seven." Then Elana used her assertiveness by challenging him to do better, asking, "What would it take for you to get it just one level higher, to eight?" Karl paused for a moment and offered some improvements to his ideas. Elana then used the WWW to help him craft a specific, accountable action plan. You can see in the chart below what Karl committed to.

Who	What	When
Karl	Will apologize to the team and to Simone	Today
Karl	Will test all aspects of the technology to weed out any last minute bugs	Three days and one day before any sales demo
Karl	Will research and present Elana with his prioritized list of professional development opportunities	Next Wednesday

As the conversation was ending, Karl and Elana committed to reinstituting their monthly one-on-ones, which had fallen by the wayside. These meetings would enable Elana to continue to coach Karl and support him in the change and in his career.

There are a few things in this conversation that Elana did especially well. The first thing was that she was genuinely curious, and wanted to resolve the problem and anything that might have been driving it. If you could have seen the conversation, you might have noticed how well her body language worked in this situation. She was sitting upright with an open posture, slightly leaning forward. Also, her body language and verbal language were congruent. Incongruence is where many conversations derail—for example, when a leader is about to confront someone but they're all smiles. Perhaps this is from nervousness and not wanting to be mean, but it sends mixed signals to the other person.

Elana, on the other hand, had a slightly concerned look on her face, and it matched her directness in talking about the issue. But she wasn't aggressive. When the conversation got to the inquiry part, she lightened up a bit and leaned in a bit more and gave him time to respond. All the way through the conversation, her body language was congruent with her words.

But what if the person gets defensive? It's likely that they will, to differing degrees. It's a natural reaction to feel defensive when presented with feedback. People perceive feedback as a threat, and because of how humans are wired, we react as if it's a physical threat. For some, this is driven by a fear of failure and/or the fear of rejection. Others fear that any little thing that goes wrong is a threat to their most basic ability to survive and pay for their food and shelter. So when facilitating a challenging conversation, don't be surprised if they have some degree of defensive reaction.

So, what do you do when faced with defensive reactions? Here are three ways to work with defensiveness.

I. **Empathy.** Let them know that you hear them. Paraphrase what they're saying so they know that you know. Have "thick-skinned empathy," so you're understanding without necessarily agreeing.

2. **Be the adult.** I've yet to see a parenting book that recommends that parents join in on a tantrum with a toddler. It's the same thing at work. If the person you're working with gets significantly defensive, be the adult; don't join in. Maintain your professional composure and stay calm, but not detached or stoic. Furthermore, don't tell them to calm down; that will likely trigger worse behavior, as they may take it as you either not agreeing about the significance of what you're talking about, or that you're belittling them in a parental way.

3. **Have a strong resolve to solve.** Resolve translates into resilience when you get the pushback of defensiveness. Be resolved to keep the conversation focused on the issue that you want to discuss. When people get defensive, they're also in biological fight-or-flight mode, meaning that they have "brain drain" because the blood has left the brain to go to the extremities, and they're pumped full of adrenaline. One of the ways to help them is to be patient, provide empathy, and let the fight-or-flight reaction subside.

While the above tips will work with most people in most situations, there are still times when you need to take a break, and that's okay. If you do, find a time within the hour to reconvene and finish the conversation. If someone is so volatile and unstable, it would be wise to involve other people just for the sake of safety, even if they're just outside the door.

Summary

Savvy Leaders know the importance of conversations to their results. They also understand that different situations require different levels of assertiveness and pivots in the conversation. They use the 5 i Conversation model to provide frequent coaching feedback, solve problems with individuals or teams and confront when necessary.

Action Steps

- Think back on a challenging workplace conversation in your past. Break down how well—or poorly—it followed the 5 i Conversational Model. Can that conversation be easily broken down into the five Is, or was it more random?

- More importantly, consider how helpful that conversation was in terms of results. Decide what you could have done differently to make the conversation more effective.

- Identify at least one challenging conversation you know you need to have. Break that conversation down using the 5 i Model and create a script for how the conversation should flow.

- Now put that script into action. If you like, write a bulleted list of key statements you want to be sure you make.

- Most importantly, rinse and repeat often—because productive conversations are the lifeblood of Savvy Leadership.

CHAPTER 11
Leadership Redefined

This book isn't just a book; it's a powerful playbook of Savvy Leadership that enhances engagement and drives high performance. When you bring the core elements of Savvy Leadership together, it creates an amazing synergy—just like those 96 little ten horsepower motors moving the 22-million-pound Safeco Field roof. One of those motors, or even a bunch of them, couldn't do it; but using them all in concert with each other creates a tipping point where they can make the move happen.

This happens in sports when you get a team "clicking on all cylinders," meaning they've developed their technical competence to a high level and have created a team synergy that propels them to succeed, even when faced with adversity and situations where other teams would have not succeeded. As a leader, whether by title or not, you have the same potential. How you lead matters, and it will dictate what you're able to accomplish.

A Savvy Leader understands that their mindset and each of their interactions feed into the dynamic that they establish with their team and collaborators. The three major dynamic curves that we talked about in the first chapter were Engagement, Compliance, and Headwinds. The most common dynamic curves are Compliance and Headwinds. It's the rare leader who knows how to activate the latent engagement potential within people. They do it by being savvy about how they lead. They have proactively adjusted their defaults, whereas others are happy to leave their defaults where it feels comfortable, and claim, "I'm just being true to who I am."

The defaults of a Savvy Leader are just that: defaults. In the game of basketball, players are taught "the stance," which is the way to position your body to defend, shoot, dribble, or pass. It's their default and is highly effective in most situations. Once you've programmed your default and practiced it, it's easier to make effective adjustments and pivot from the stance.

Savvy Leaders are cognizant of their customized default, and we've covered that throughout this book as well as a number of key concepts required to drive the engagement curve dynamic. So let's bring it together and look at the defaults.

1. **Increases Awareness:** Savvy Leaders are always building their awareness in key areas of cultural awareness, situational awareness, and people awareness. This helps inform them of what is real and how to interpret it. That, in turn, informs them regarding what adjustments to make as they lead. Without awareness, leadership can feel more like "fire, aim, ready" than "ready, aim, fire."

2. **Enhancing Engagement:** Savvy Leaders understand that engagement is their responsibility, as they are the most significant variable in affecting it, and it doesn't change without proactive, intentional, consistent action. They set their defaults to strong relational and motivational engagement, and ensure that they're modeling engagement as well.

3. **Reducing Headwinds:** To drive for results, leaders need to use power and influence, but Savvy Leaders know what types of power and influence to use to drive the engagement curve and results. They set their power defaults to primarily developing and using Expert and Referent Power, and only using other types of power when necessary. Their influence defaults build on Expert and Referent Power, and include a primary emphasis on Rational Persuasion, with a secondary emphasis on Inspirational Appeals, Consultation, and Collaboration. By doing so, they're able to influence others better with or without authority, as they're able to sway both the hearts and minds of those they're leading. Only when needed, and only for a short time, do they use their Positional Power or any of the harder influence tactics. Then, they revert right back to their savvy defaults.

4. **Optimizing for Results:** Savvy Leaders understand that there are often just a few degrees of separation between success and failure. To improve their odds of getting over the tipping point to their results goal, they hone their assertiveness and communication. In particular, they set their assertiveness default to proactive assertiveness. They advocate in a respectful but forward manner, without crossing the line into being disrespectful and aggressive. The only times they deviate from that posture is when the team needs to be more empowered, or when accomplishing the goal requires a very rare and momentary shot of aggressiveness. They dial in their assertiveness to overcome obstacles and develop their talent by frequently using the 5 i Conversation Model and the pivots for coaching feedback and confrontation.

While there are certainly other areas a leader can grow in, if their defaults aren't set to Savvy Leadership, not much else will matter—

because it's not as much *what* you lead but *how* you lead that will determine the outcome. Many have asked me at what level this type of learning is needed. In my experience, this is helpful from novice all the way up to the highest levels of leadership, and the lack of this understanding is why engagement rates suffer and work results are stifled. The important thing to note here is that a title alone doesn't make you an effective leader, but knowing the playbook of Savvy Leadership can. That's true whether you're in college, working as an intern, a volunteer, an individual contributor, a leader, or a senior leader. As people climb the ladder, it's tempting to get "fancy" with leadership development and it often results in minimal gains if the components of Savvy Leadership aren't already in place.

Just like in professional sports, a leader may be advanced in their talent, but basketball players still practice shooting, and soccer players still practice dribbling. If the core abilities aren't effective, nothing else matters. I once heard about a pastor who kept preaching the same pithy sermon week after week. Eventually, after his fourth time preaching the same sermon, one of the parishioners confronted the pastor about it. The pastor replied, "I'll stop preaching it when people start doing it." The same is true with Savvy Leadership. You can't emphasize enough how important this is to driving engagement and results.

How you lead matters. It matters deep inside of you; it matters to your organization, your colleagues, and their families, and it matters to your results. You now have a powerful playbook to put it into action, to make amazing things happen. I'll be cheering you on!

Ben Zander, the conductor of the Boston Philharmonic Orchestra, summed it up well:

One way to check whether I'm doing an adequate job is to look in my musicians' eyes. The eyes never lie. If the eyes are shining, then I know that my leadership is working. Human beings in the presence of possibility react physically as well as emotionally. If the eyes aren't shining, I ask myself, "What am I doing that is keeping my musicians' eyes from shining?" [29]

Now, more than ever, we need more shining eyes in the world. *You* are the biggest variable in making that happen, because how you lead truly matters.

RESOURCES

- Author Q & A
- Leadership Planner

Author Q & A

Why did you name it "Savvy"?

I found that savvy best describes the types of leaders who can deliver high performance even in changing circumstances with many variables. Savvy connotes an acquired kind of knowledge that is more closely aligned with practical intelligence than with IQ.

Why did you choose to write one book that covers so many concepts instead of spreading it out over several books?

I wanted to create a book packed full of value, but also make it brief enough so that you could easily read the whole book on one airplane flight and land with a whole new way of leading. To do that I have found that most people don't need to know everything about each subject. Instead, they need to know what the concept is, why it works, how to use it, and an example to illustrate it. They also need a framework to connect the concepts together — in this book, the overarching concept is Savvy Leadership and how each part impacts the J-curve dynamics.

I also wanted to break away from the common paradigm of focusing on one dimension. Though I know the promise of "one thing" sells books, it does so at the expense of oversimplifying leadership. If you have studied human beings long enough, particularly effective leaders, you realize that there is more than one thing that drives their effectiveness. It's multi-dimensional.

How can I use this book to be more effective as a leader?

The first step is awareness. By reading this book, you become aware of what to look for and then how to adjust. In the back of the book is a sample form that you can use to guide the application of the concepts to your real world situations. You can also visit our website at www.savvyleader.com and download (for free) the same form as a fillable PDF form. I encourage you to use it yourself and also to use it to help coach other people. I've yet to find a simpler, more effective tool. If you find one, let me know!

What if I want to bring this leadership approach to my organization?

I loved writing this book mainly because it makes the Savvy Leadership approach accessible to anyone, not just the people in our workshops. If you want to go deeper and receive hands-on training on the concepts in this book, then I encourage you to explore our services by visiting our website (www.savvyleadership.com) or by giving us a call. Our primary offering is the one-day workshop based on the content in this book, but we also offer consulting to ensure that there is a strong transfer of learning and impact on results. Train the trainer certification is available for those who want to facilitate the workshop within their own organization.

Wait, did you just say a one-day workshop?

Yes! In the modern workplace, organizations just don't have the time anymore to spend a whole week on the subjects covered in the Savvy

Leadership Workshop, but it doesn't need to take that long to be effective. My philosophy is to give you just what you need to know about each concept to make it practical and relevant. In addition to learning a new leadership playbook, each participant in our workshop leaves with a detailed strategy sheet applying what they learned to a real situation in which they need to lead.

If we already have a leadership development program at our organization, how would this fit in?

I'd have to know more about the programs you have. In most cases, the Savvy Leadership program enhances what is already in place and connects the dots between programs that are typically disconnected. The Savvy Leadership program can often replace a week's worth of training and streamline it to just one day with structured follow-up to ensure it sticks. This saves time, money, and energy.

Who is Savvy Leadership intended for?

It is for everyone who has to influence others to reach a goal. That is pretty much everyone in life. I've had frontline workers tell me "No one has ever explained this stuff to me before. Thank you! I'm going to use this!" and I've had senior leaders say "I've heard some parts of this before but never have I seen it all pulled together and put into a playbook that I can start using immediately!" It's for people in corporate jobs and for people in education and non-profits who are working with volunteers. Having worked in student development at a university, this certainly works for students who are graduating and moving into their first job (think about the advantage they would have on day one if they already knew the methodology for becoming a savvy leader at their organization!).

How do you set this program up for a successful implementation?

In my experience, when people truly put to work the concepts in this book to work, it greatly increases their odds of successfully achieving their goal. It doesn't guarantee it, but it puts the odds in their favor. When it comes to implementing this program in an organization, there a few pitfalls that the organization should ensure that they don't fall into.

The first pitfall is thinking that a workshop is a one-day event. If you treat it that way, you won't gain the traction and ROI that you could. Instead, savvy organizations turn it into a campaign that begins before the workshop occurs by getting the participants ready for what they are going to be challenged with. Then afterward, there needs to be a simple structure in place to ensure that follow through on what was learned in the classroom happens back on the job.

The second pitfall is not having the senior leaders champion the new way of leading. If they fail to sponsor, attend, model or follow through on it, then they are setting an example through their actions that it's not important. Sometimes it's better to do nothing than to do training that's not supported because that can breed cynicism. If you are going to make the investment to train people, then part of your plan has to be to getting visible senior leadership championing this new way of leading.

The third pitfall is not measuring and rewarding the new behavior. I'm always delighted when I hear organizations say that they measure the performance of their people, not only by what they produce, but how they produce it. The people who do both well are the ones who are rewarded and promoted.

Anything else?

This work is my passion. If more people had the type of leadership savvy that we describe in this book, not only would organizations get better results, but we could transform the workplace into an environment where people shine because of how their leader is leading. I am all in on making that the new reality! If you are too, then let's talk.

Leadership Planner

(Visit www.savvyleadership.com to download a free fillable PDF version of the Leadership Planner.)

SITUATION & GOAL

Situation (What is the situation in which you need to lead?)

Goal (What is your goal in this situation?)

AWARENESS
(Develop your awareness so that you can make savvy adjustments)

Cultural (What approaches to change and leadership work well in this organizational culture?)

People (Who is involved and what is their personality? What adjustments should you make?)

ENGAGEMENT
(Strengthen goodwill and improve discretionary effort level)

Relational (List two things you can do to enhance relational engagement with key people involved.)

Motivational (List specific ways you can incorporate the P.E.D. of Motivational Engagement.)

REDUCING HEADWINDS
(Create a dynamic that makes it easier to move forward)

Power (List which types of power you will emphasize as you navigate to your goal.)

Influence (Write out how you will apply any of the core four influence tactics to your situation.)

OPTIMIZING FOR RESULTS
(Increase the odds of reaching your goal)

Preparation (List what you need to do in advance of moving forward.)

Assertiveness (At what level do you need to set your assertiveness?)

Conversations (List at least two specific conversations you need to have to reach your goal.)

ACTION PLAN
(List at least four specific items to reach your goal.
Include deadlines for action.)

About the Author

CAM TRIPP

Cam is the founder and CEO of Savvy Leadership, LLC, a leadership development company focused on transforming leaders and organizations with the concepts presented in this book. He received his Masters Degree in Counseling Psychology from Trinity Evangelical Divinity School in Deerfield, Il in the 1990's. While there, he noticed that many of the people in his classes were ministers who had returned and were auditing psychology classes to better understand and lead people in their congregations. That observation sparked his interest and led to a career developing healthy, effective, engaging leaders.

Throughout his career consulting, facilitating and delivering keynotes, Cam has had the opportunity to partner with hundreds of organizations including Fortune 500 companies, SMBs, educational institutions, non-profits and government agencies. His experiences behind the scenes provided clear insights into what was really needed to rapidly develop leaders who simultaneously enhance engagement and drive high-performance in the modern workplace. He wrote Savvy Leadership to inspire great leadership and provide a simple, practical roadmap for how to actually do it.

Outside of work he can be found on the sidelines coaching his kids' sports teams near Seattle or exploring the mountains and waterways of the great Pacific Northwest with his family.

Endnotes

1. Jim Harter and Amy Adkins, 2015. "Employees Want a Lot More from Their Managers," *Gallup Business Journal.* Online at http://www.gallup.com/businessjournal/182321/employees-lot-managers.aspx. Retrieved March 9, 2016.

2. Safeco Field Facts and Ground Rules. Online at http://seattle.mariners.mlb.com/sea/ballpark/information/index.jsp?content=facts. Retrieved March 9, 2016.

3. Tim Waters, Robert J. Marzano, and Brian McNulty. "Balanced Leadership: What 30 Years of Research Tells Us about the Effect of Leadership on Student Achievement. A Working Paper." Mid-Continent Regional Education Lab, Aurora, Colorado. Online at http://eric.ed.gov/?id=ED481972. Retrieved March 9, 2016.

4. Daniel Goleman. *Emotional Intelligence: Why It Can Matter More Than IQ.* New York: Bantam Books, 2005.

5. "Big Five Personality Traits," Wikipedia. Online at https://en.wikipedia.org/wiki/Big_Five_personality_traits. Retrieved March 9, 2016.

6. To learn more about the five-factor model and how it applies to leadership and work, I recommend you read: Jane Mitchell Howard and Pierce Howard, *The Owner's Manual for Personality at Work: How the Big Five Personality Traits Affect Performance, Communication, Teamwork, Leadership, and Sales,* 2nd Edition. Charlotte, NC: Center for Applied Cognitive Studies, 2010.

7. "70% of U.S. Workers Not Engaged at Work," State of the American Workplace Report. Gallup Online, at http://www.gallup.com/services/178514/state-american-workplace.aspx?g_source=position4&g_medium=related&g_campaign=tiles. Retrieved March 9, 2016.

8. Wendy Levinson et al., "Physician-Patient Communication: The Relationship with Malpractice Claims Among Primary Care Physicians and Surgeons." *JAMA, the Journal of the American Medical Association* 277(7):553-559, January 1997.

9. Kim Therese Buehlman, John Mordecai Gottman, and Lyne Fainsilber Katz. "How a Couple Views Their Past Predicts Their Future: Predicting Divorce from an Oral History Interview." Journal of Family Psychology, Vol. 5, No. 3 & 4, March/June 1992: 295-318;

   and

   Ellie Lisitsa. "The Positive Perspective: Dr. Gottman's Magic Ratio!" The Gottman Institute Blog, December 5, 2012. Online at https://www.gottman.com/blog/the-positive-perspective-dr-gottmans-magic-ratio/. Retrieved March 9, 2016.

10. 10 Simon Sinek, "How Great Leaders Inspire Action." September 2009. TED Talk for the TED Institute. Online at https://www.ted.com/talks/simon_sinek_how_great_leaders_inspire_action?language=en. Retrieved March 9, 2016.

11. Alexandra Levit with Dr. Sanja Licina. "How the Recession Shaped Millennial and Hiring Manager Attitudes about Millennials' Future Careers." Career Advisory Board, 2012. Online at http://www.careeradvisoryboard.org/public/uploads/2011/10/Future-of-Millennial-Careers-Report.pdf. Retrieved March 9, 2016.

12. Adam Grant, "How Customers Can Rally Your Troops." *Harvard Business Review*, June 2011. Online at https://hbr.org/2011/06/how-customers-can-rally-your-troops. Retrieved March 9, 2016.

13. Christine Porath. "Half of Employees Don't Feel Respected by Their Bosses." *Harvard Business Review*, November 2014.

14. Mihaly Csikzentmihaly, *Flow: The Psychology of Optimal Experience.* Harper and Row: New York, 1990.

15. "French and Raven's bases of power." Wikipedia, online at https://en.wikipedia.org/wiki/French_and_Raven%27s_bases_of_power. Retrieved March 9, 2016.

16. Adapted from Gary A. Yukl, *Leadership in Organizations,* 7th edition. Pearson Education Inc., Upper Saddle River. NJ: 2010.

17. Keith Danko, "General Management, Inspiring Others." SmartBlog on Leadership, Online at http://smartblogs.com/leadership/2014/11/21/tough-is-easy/. March 9, 2016.

18. Yukl, *Leadership in Organizations*.

19. David Kipnis, Stuart M. Schmidt, Chris Swaffin-Smith, and Ian F. Wilkinson. "Patterns of Managerial Influence: Shotgun Managers, Tacticians, and Bystanders." Organizational Dynamics 12(3), S. 59-67.

20. Yukl, *Leadership in Organizations*.

21. *Ibid.*

22. Aner Tal and Brian Wansink. "Blinded with science: Trivial graphs and formulas increase ad persuasiveness and belief in product efficacy." *Public Understanding of Science.* January 2016, 25(1): 117-125.

23. E.J. Langer, A. Blank, and B. Chanowitz, "The mindlessness of ostensibly thoughtful action: the role of "placebic" information in interpersonal interaction." *Journal of Personality and Social Psychology* 36(3): 635-642.

24. Katie Liljenquist and Adam D. Galinsky. "Win Over an Opponent by Asking for Advice." *Harvard Business Review*, June 2014. Online at https://hbr.org/2014/06/win-over-an-opponent-by-asking-for-advice. Retrieved March 9, 2016.

25. Heidi Grant Halvorson. "Managers Can motivate Employees with One Word." *Harvard Business Review*, August 2014. Online at https://hbr.org/2014/08/managers-can-motivate-employees-with-one-word/. March 9, 2016.

26. Daniel Ames, "Pushing up to a point: Assertiveness and effectiveness in leadership and interpersonal dynamics." *Research in Organizational Behavior* 29 (2009) 111–133.

27. Joseph Folkman and Jack Zenger, "Nice or Tough: Which Approach Engages Employees Most?" Harvard Business Review, September 2013. Online at https://hbr.org/2013/09/nice-or-tough-what-engages-emp/. Retrieved March 9, 2016.

28. O'Neill, O. A. and O'Reilly III, C. A. (2011), "Reducing the backlash effect: Self-monitoring and women's promotions." Journal of Occupational and Organizational Psychology, 84: 825–832.

29. Labarre, Polly (1998, December). Leadership - Ben Zander. Fast Company

INDEX

SERVICES

Keynotes: Use a Savvy Leadership Keynote to kick off your next conference or event. Our keynotes inspire audiences to view leadership in a new and powerful way that focus on creating the dynamics for performance no matter what the challenge is.

Workshops: The Savvy Leadership Workshop is a highly interactive one-day experience. Participants learn the concepts of Savvy Leadership and apply them to their current work challenges. Each participant leaves the workshop with a new leadership playbook and a custom, detailed plan to lead toward a specific business result while inspiring authentic engagement and igniting high performance.

Transfer of Learning: The finish line is not when the workshop is over, but is several months down the road when behavioral change is taking root and measurable results are showing up. The best way to drive the transfer of learning is to equip team leaders with simple, quick, effective ways to continue to challenge their teams to use what they learned. Each leader receives access to our password protected online resources to enable leader-led change.

Train the Trainer Certification: Many organizations already have excellent facilitators on their teams. We can partner with them so they can deliver the workshop within their own organization. Certifying internal trainers provides a more organizationally connected session, embedded learning sustainability, and cost-savings. For those times when you want outside expertise, we are available to provide facilitation.

Learn more on our website: www.SavvyLeadership.com

Referrals: Referrals are the lifeblood of our business. We work hard to deliver world-class solutions to every client. If you know of an organization that could benefit from our work, we would welcome an introduction. The easiest way to make the virtual introduction is to email us your name, email and your referral's contact information.

You can email us at referral@savvyleadership.com. Thank you in advance!

NOTES

NOTES

Proof

Made in the USA
Charleston, SC
02 October 2016